36
WAYS
TO HAVE A HAPPY
SEX
LIFE

To Barnaby, Joel and Alexander

365

—WAYS—
TO HAVE A HAPPY

SEX

—LIFE—

Answers to all those questions you've always wanted to ask!

PHILLIP HODSON
& ANNE HOOPER

Thorsons Publishing Group

First published 1990

British Library Cataloguing in Publication Data

Hodson, Phillip
   365 ways to have a happy sex life.
   1. Sex relations.
   I. Title   II. Hooper, Anne
   306.7

   ISBN 0-7225-1871-4

Published by Thorsons Publishers Limited, Wellingborough, Northamptonshire NN8 2RQ, England

Typeset by Harper Phototypesetters Limited, Northampton, England
Printed in Great Britain by Mackays, Chatham, Kent

10 9 8 7 6 5 4 3 2

Contents

Introduction

Well, you could try swinging from a chandelier with a carrot in each ear and a nose full of amyl nitrite, watching a blue movie on your wall projector while fantasizing about Uncle Barnabas in his Death's Head uniform surrounded by naked slave ballerinas chorusing from the *Story of O*, but we reckon you've got a bit beyond that. The more you pile on sensation, the less you feel. The more you search for kicks, the more you hunger for hugs. The more detached you feel about pleasure, the less you care if it occurs.

Sex as an act of repeated consumption ceases to gratify. Georges Simenon, the late crime writer, is reputed to have had 10,000 women in his adult lifetime. That's more than three females weekly, 52 weeks a year for 61 years. Curiously, sex for Simenon never seemed to achieve penetration. Yes, he had intercourse. But the act never got through to him. It remained external, mechanical, an essay in human asset-stripping and he played the supreme accountant. And yet according to the encyclopaedias of love and sex, he did it by the book. Foreplay preceded intromission and was in turn succeeded by afterplay. Altogether, a highly accomplished lover, they would suggest.

It seems to us that what have often been missing from 'sex manuals' are human beings. Bodies don't have sex. Personalities have sex, but not in isolation. Sex, when it isn't by yourself, actually takes place between personalities in relationships, however briefly, however commercially. In this setting, feelings predominate. This provides one of our reasons for producing a book based on many years' counselling in the consulting room and listening on radio to strangers talking about their problems. The differences between men and women, whether conditioned or not, figure significantly. But our main effort is to try to explain in question-and-answer form the secrets of personal emotional growth that will increase your sexual pleasure.

Sex in the 1990s is not just about physical sexual problems or coping with the aftermath of Victorian repression and getting laid. Within the limits of an AIDS culture, we are currently faced with more choices than problems. On the whole, people now feel comfortable with the sexual mechanics (and the exceptions still make interesting questions). Where we start to feel anxious is about our own psychology: 'Why do I feel the way I do? Not just about my sexual desires, but also about my jealousies, depressions, tantrums, rages, fears, my hostility and vulnerability beneath and alongside those desires?'

If we're honest, we'll probably admit that sex life cannot be 'privatized' or set to make a profit ('I've had more partners than you'). It cannot be run in isolation from thoughts, feelings, past history, memory, fantasy and family conditioning — in effect the total 'emotional state' in which we find ourselves. The reason why desire fades, two-thirds of impotence problems begin, spouses have headaches, intercourse is disappointing or gin bottles get drained in nearly always the same — not physical waning but emotional drowning. We feel bad because of the troubled state of our 'inner' selves, a world which some in America have reduced to superficiality but too many in Britain can barely locate on their mental maps. As one young Englishman wrote: 'Why did I fail with this bird I didn't fancy a bit but needed to give it a go with in order to keep my sex life up to scratch?' Or going further up-market: 'I will pay you £10,000 if you can offer me a reliable method of extending my six-inch penis by four inches.'

We also feel time has been unkind to some of the better manuals of the past. Eighteen years ago, Alex Comfort in *The Joy of Sex* felt free to state: 'Sex must be physically the safest of all human activities . . . It won't make you obese or atherosclerotic, or give you ulcers.' The only hazards he feared were minor but preventable — for example, in 1972, all known venereal diseases could be successfully cured. He did state that you should avoid the risk of 'accidental sexual murder' — blowing into a woman's vagina was (and remains) a bad idea, since it can cause air embolism, fooling around with vacuum cleaners could be sexually dangerous — suction occasionally leading to section. But all in all his seven paragraphs on 'Hazards' conclude: 'Given reasonable gentleness, sex play is by far the safest energetic sport — one can be killed dead by a golf ball . . . The worst sex can make you is sore, anxious or disappointed.'

Obviously, it is more than time to update such views. Sexually transmitted virus is today the leading cause of death for adults aged under 35 in New York. A pandemic of AIDS or 'slim's disease' is raging in Africa. And even if most Westerners thankfully do not yet permit the fear of death to spoil all their erotic joy, it has crossed everyone's mind that sex can kill. This in itself has been enough to reduce the force of libido in some lives. Unconscious fear may lie behind some quite conscious anger about adultery and infidelity. 'Open' marriage is less the fashion than it was when the O'Neills wrote their best-selling book (again in 1972). Group sex parties do not hold the significance accorded to them by Dr Comfort. The headline-pushing Dr Martin Cole admits his clinics can no longer prescribe 'surrogate therapy' as an acceptable method of treatment. And according to a press report, the drains of North London in 1989 were more frequently clogged with discarded condoms than with any other item of household refuse. Certainly far more than they were when Alex Comfort damned these miniature life-jackets (Mae Wests?) with faint praise in his textbook as 'still having their uses'.

This being so, now more than ever we need to look at sex honestly. In relationships, it helps make us what we are. It helps bond and bind us to each other. It gives us information about ourselves we can get in no other way. And it does not need to be sacrificed on the altar of disease. Rather, sex must be adapted to the circumstances in which it finds itself. Sex is always about touch, and often about orgasm. Neither of these resolutely require penetration, which can in any case be made safer, so why give sex a bad name?

This book is divided into natural phases of life beginning with the relationships of young couples, seeing what happens when children become more sexually aware, examining times of crisis and divorce, going on to the transformation of teenagers into lovers, exploring mid-life, looking at sexual 'specialities' in their context and the hoped-for sexual wisdom of old age. Our only wish is that, whatever you think of the book, you like the subject more after reading it.

1 The young couple in bed

Q **My vulva always feels wet. My boyfriend says I must be a nymphomaniac but I tell him I don't feel madly sexy all the time.**

A Quite — and normal vulvas *are* moist, receiving routine lubrication from Bartholin's gland. As Alex Comfort once remarked: 'Of course they are. If it weren't so, women would squeak when they walk!' Note: nymphomaniacs hardly exist. This is a term used by men to describe women who behave like one of the boys.

Q **How often do people normally have sex per day? My boyfriend and I made love 11 times on the first day of our first holiday.**

A Well, we're happy for you. In the early flush of a relationship, it's common for lovers to couple several times daily as part of the process of bonding. Sex is shorthand for 'I love you and I want to get you under my skin'. But it would be straining convention to describe 11 separate acts of intercourse as typical. Of course, you might mean '11 orgasms during one act of sex' (possible for the woman) or you might mean '11 couplings without orgasm at all' (managed daily by live sex show performers in the clubs of Hamburg and Amsterdam). It would certainly be very difficult for a man to ejaculate 11 times during a 24-hour period, whatever his age, though he might manage a number of eventual 'dry comes'. The largest claim we ever heard made was from a teenage Hungarian couple who said they had sex 16 times on their wedding night, but who can prove what? Your question suggests quantity is almost causing you anxiety. Inevitably, as time goes by, you will learn not to 'count the bouts' but to enjoy the bond. Couples usually exaggerate how often they make love, although the married average is claimed to be just two or three times weekly.

Q My girlfriend is very nervous about sex unless she has a drink first. Then she becomes a different woman and encourages me outrageously. But she never seems to have an orgasm.

A Alcohol works by depressing your inhibitions. If you drink several units, quite large areas of brain activity will get depressed. Drink more, and eventually you will lose motor control. The relationship between sex and alcohol, therefore, is a complicated equation of 'how much, how quickly and who's doing the drinking?' Your girlfriend is anxious about sexuality. She gets Dutch courage from gin or vodka and liberates her fantasies. But her anxieties are too strong to permit climax and if she gets drunk she won't function at all.

The answer, therefore, is to explore her worries. Does she need to get to know you better in order to trust you? Is she inexperienced and therefore naturally afraid of the psychological risks of new behaviour? Is she anxious about orgasm itself? Is she scared of 'letting go' for reasons of trauma? Was she ever attacked or raped, sexually abused, derided or criticized? Did her parents suggest sex was filthy and all boys brutes? Does she have strong religious inhibitions? Or is she simply not being stimulated enough by you to get turned on? Please ask *her* these questions.

Q I fear I am letting my lover down badly by not being able to climax at the same time as him. I can manage it before or after but I am so busy concentrating on him I can't focus my mind on myself and he is getting angry with me.

A His anger makes things worse. Coming together is always easier said than done. In effect, the 'tyranny' of simultaneous orgasm was invented by mystic sex educators together with novelists like D. H. Lawrence earlier in this century. Thus Dr Wright in her *Sex Factor in Marriage* (1930):

As the act proceeds, the intensity of pleasure rises, thought is abandoned, a curious feeling of the spirit, very difficult to describe, takes place. It is as if there were, hidden among the sensations of the body, a spiritual counterpart, a pleasure of soul, only attained for a few seconds, bringing with it a dazzling glimpse of the Unity which underlies all nature. The rhythm of movement becomes quicker, the breathing deeper, the sensation of pleasure more and more intense, until both the man and woman together reach a climax . . . no couple should be content until they have learnt how to experience orgasm together.

In fact, sexual intercourse is not a contest fixed to end in a dead heat. Biology is against simultaneity. Not for nothing is orgasm called *La Petite Mort* – the little death. What happens as you approach climax is that your consciousness alters. Sometimes, you get completely tuned out. It only takes a small change in the rhythm of your lovemaking for your partner to lose his or her own climax. How on earth can you be a good lover if you yourself are being forced to abandon muscle control and presence of mind? Your boyfriend needs a bit of 're-education' on this score. Tell him he's actually spoiling what sounds like an excellent sexual partnership. You can also tell him many prefer to enjoy climax separately because, as Bernie Zilbergeld reported, 'non-simultaneous sex nearly always results in stronger sensation' (*Men and Sex*, 1978). Moreover, the goal of joint climax ignores the woman's ability to have multiple orgasms. Very few men are so endowed. This being so, it makes sense, as Leo Durocher once wrote about the New York Giants, for 'nice guys to finish last'.

Q **I feel such a fool because I fake orgasm. I've read in all the books that this is pointless but I can't seem to stop myself. Why do I go on doing it?**

A Clearly you fear your lover will reject you if you cannot respond to him orgasmically. If he is a vulnerable, unstable character you have instinctively decided that faking with him is sensible and, for exactly the same reasons, having a proper orgasm in his company would feel too risky. Then again, maybe you have other anxieties about sex for which he is the innocent focus? Maybe you have enjoyed a feeling of power too by being able to deceive him very easily and you fear losing this if you tell him the truth. Almost inevitably, improving a relationship means taking risks. Either life with him is always going to be pretty joyless or the problem is mainly in you. Whichever, it is to your advantage to break the pattern now by voicing discontents and fears. If you can masturbate to orgasm alone, you could teach him how to do this for you. If he won't assist, then the relationship itself seems in question.

Q **I daren't let myself climax with my new man because I know I go bright red in the face, groan and look terrible. How do others manage to let go?**

A By realizing that most of us go scarlet, contort and grunt when we come. Take a peek at your bloke when he does. You could help yourself by keeping the lights down low and asking for more reassurance. Since most men are excited when their partners climax, we expect he will co-operate.

Q **When I climax I pee and I am very embarrassed. I cope with this when masturbating by covering myself with towels, but I can't bring myself to do this with my boyfriend. So far I've stopped myself from climaxing but it's getting astonishingly difficult. My man is a marvellous lover and I'm rigid with tension from holding out. No man is going to want to be peed on, is he?**

A Depends on the man. Some would be uncomfortable but fresh urine is sterile and completely hygienic. If your man knows this and likes the sweaty wetness of sex, he won't care. There is even a minority of men who would see your urination as a complete bonus because it turns them on. In any case, no great quantity of liquid is likely to be involved. Since your man is such a marvellous lover, we suggest he can probably cope.

Q **Why does my husband always turn the light off when we have sex? He'll leave it on if I ask but it seems to make him nervous.**

A Somehow it is easier for you to put this question to strangers like us than to the man with whom you live. So the first point is how to raise the level of communication in your marriage. Have you asked him to speak to you about all this?

Obviously, he may be shy, he may have insecurities about his body, he may associate sex in the light with illicit activity, even prostitution, or he may find darkness helpful when using fantasies during lovemaking. But *we* cannot know.

Q **It takes my partner ages (well 40 minutes at least) to reach climax. By the time she gets there I'm worn out and hardly able to keep going. Now that we're living together, how can I build up more stamina?**

A Swimming and push-ups might help. But learning to be more careful about the timing of intercourse is equally significant. Organize this in two ways. First, if the day ahead is important workwise, postpone lovemaking altogether, then have a leisurely wallow at the weekend. Secondly, when in bed, consciously prolong foreplay till your partner is near the 'point of no return'. Doing this will naturally shorten the duration of intercourse necessary for her to reach climax. (You could even consider using a vibrator as part of the fun if she is willing.) Experiment with sexual positions too (such as side-by-side) so that physical effort is reduced or at least shared. It is possible that since you are now living together, she will in any case feel more relaxed about sex and able to respond more swiftly.

Q My partner always seizes on the first second or my orgasm as a signal to have his. This is upsetting me, partly because his movements actually distract me from my orgasm and partly because I know I'm capable of more than one. But he never gives me the chance. How can I get him to last longer?

A Well, even if you think you've explained all this before, say it again so there's no doubt he knows what you require. Then if he refuses to alter his approach, you can be sure you're receiving either an aggressive or a contemptuous message, and can consider whether you wish to continue in such an unrewarding partnership. If, on the other hand, *he can't wait but would like to*, the 'squeeze' technique might prove useful. When he's near to orgasm, you interrupt sex to pinch, between your first two fingers and thumbs, the head of his penis just below the penis-crown, applying moderate to strong pressure, counting to three, and his erection should subside. With tender stroking, his erection should return and lovemaking can be resumed. Alternatively, during intercourse, pull gently on his testicles and scrotum to prevent them rising towards his body – a man finds ejaculation very difficult unless his balls are retracted by muscle reflex like an undercarriage snug against his pelvic base. However, remember that sex and perfection rarely combine. If he cannot last till your fourth and fifth orgasms, do compromise with masturbation.

Q **My boyfriend swears he can have more than one orgasm in a row and he certainly seemed to do that the other night. Is he kidding me?**

A No. Most young men can enjoy one to three orgasms within an hour or so, and many older men retain the ability. However, with age, the 'refractory' period (time between getting erections) does become more lengthy. By compensation, mature males usually possess an increased ability to defer first ejaculation.

Q **My first boyfriend made love in such a way that he stimulated my vagina with his penis at a very particular angle which always made me climax. How can I get my new lover to do the same?**

A Some lovers are tall, some short. Some men have thick blunt erections, some have sinuous spiny ones. No two people fit together as they would fit with others. Perhaps the proportions of your first man's penis suited you exquisitely. Perhaps the angle of entry was ideal. Perhaps making love with him in (say) the missionary position gave you perfect pressure on the clitoris or the anterior wall of the vagina or on the cervix. However, you cannot reasonably expect your good fortune to continue with others. You will now have to explain your needs, experiment with different positions and conceivably make do with compromise strokes and touches. For example, if you need a direct caress of the clitoris during intercourse, it is possible for either of you to introduce 'magic' fingers between your bodies to stimulate the part in question.

Q **Is it possible for men to fake orgasm? I have this feeling my boyfriend's mind is far away during sex and he is only doing this because he thinks I want it, and he seems very controlled when he (says he) comes.**

A There are times when lovers don't feel sexy but are still prepared to please their partners. It is also quite common for both sexes to feel interested in having intercourse yet not desperate to reach orgasm. This being so, you could be misjudging your partner's behaviour and it might be a good idea to enquire further. For instance, do you really know what sort of sex he likes best and at what times of day? Are there circumstances under which he feels mild, not overpowering, erotic interest? Give him 'permission' to talk about this. You could also ask him what are his favourite fantasies, games, clothes for sex, and so on.

To answer more narrowly, yes, of course, men can pretend to feel what they don't, just like women. Faking orgasm is more difficult for them in one sense because if they climax there ought to be a 'wet patch' somewhere but, if you lubricate copiously, even this can remain in doubt. We suspect you fear that your man is bored with you. Have you any other grounds for thinking this? Have you asked him recently? Have you ever been seriously rejected by others, so that history clouds your self-judgement? It is important to get to the bottom of this.

Of course, he could have a problem with 'delayed' orgasm anyway, with feeling nervous of letting go into orgasm, in which case giving him lots of climaxes by hand might be part of your sex therapy programme in getting him to trust you more.

Q I revel in the liquids of sex. I find the stickiness of my own vaginal juices and my lover's semen very erotic. I love our mingled sweat in the heat of passion. However, my fiancé is the opposite, and he can't wait to shower all that nectar away. Could he ever feel differently?

A It's possible, but it may take you several years of gentle re-education. Have you the patience to get him to talk about the origin and content of his physical fastidiousness? You'd need to probe the connections between his understanding of sex and hygiene. Does he think 'love juice' is somehow polluted? Does he associate sex with excretion? Does he think 'waste products' are obscene? Could he rethink them as essentially natural? Was he punished for 'dirty' thoughts, words or deeds as a little boy? Additionally, you could show him that your fluids are clean, sweet-smelling, viscous and benign. Do this when he is very aroused, rather than after orgasm, so that he begins to associate wetness with delight. You could also persuade him to delay taking a post-coital shower to provide you with the necessary holding of after-play.

Q My girlfriend often can't have an orgasm when we make love even though she gets very worked up. She insists it doesn't matter but I worry. Could she suffer physically from being unsatisfied?

A Nothing dire or dangerous will happen to her, although if she begins to suffer from pelvic tension and congestion, she could develop backache, restlessness, 'twitchy' legs and mild sleep disorder. Perhaps your girlfriend should be encouraged to practise self-pleasuring? Suggest she takes a warm bath, then gets into bed alone, with massage oil to stroke herself erotically and sensuously, perhaps mouthing favourite fantasies, and becoming accustomed to safe, sexual strokes. If she knew her own responses better, sex with you would stand an increased chance of success.

Q My boyfriend keeps his erection but can't seem to come inside me. He has to go into the bathroom to finish things off by masturbation. I feel very depressed about this.

A Either your boyfriend is not getting sufficient penile friction from intercourse to take him over the top or he has psychological difficulty in 'letting go'. If the latter, it is much more likely to have been caused by past relationships, and their emotional distress, than by anything you have said or done. Simple sex therapy for this problem makes use of the fact that he has easy orgasms by manual means, and is probably very used to the rapid, intense strokes provided by muscular fingers. Therefore the plan is as follows. Get him to share his masturbation with you. Ask him how he likes you to hold him and how you can best press, squeeze, tease and please. See if you can make him ejaculate by masturbation near your upper thighs. If it's too difficult, see if he can do this for himself. Show how willingly you accept his erection, his desire, his semen and his vulnerability after climax.

When comfortable with this stage, move on to a kind of 'mixed masturbation and intercourse' with him able to direct the scenario in order to allay his anxiety. Also ensure that when he is lodged inside you for intercourse, you choose a position that allows you to close your legs (his outside yours?) so the level of pressure between you is at a maximum. Finally, where relevant, see if he is willing to talk about any of these: his dominant mother; his bossy sister(s); his emotionally distant father; his rejecting girlfriend(s); his unpleasant sexual encounters as a child or teenager and his worst ever moments of loss or abandonment. If you can open up these areas, you will generate deeper intimacy and love.

Q My boyfriend swears sex is giving him hay fever!

A If you use unlubricated condoms he could be right. Sometimes, the powder on un-oiled sheaths contains lycopodium (pollen of the club-moss) to which many people may be allergic. Note: sex makes most of us sneeze anyway because physical arousal is rarely organ-specific — if you get turned on anywhere, your nose tends to tickle and run too.

Q **My girlfriend is very keen on experimenting with different positions. We've tried doing it standing up, sitting down and with our noses in a sex manual. Although it's been fun, I'm getting rather anxious. I'd like more routine, but she seems driven, almost desperate. What could this be about?**

A Well, isn't she trying to prove something? It sounds as though she wants to convince you as well as herself that she is a very erotic person. This being so, the good psychic detective says: 'Who once told her that she wasn't? Who once made her feel unattractive or insecure?' Find out more about her sexual background so that she can start to challenge these tape-recorded messages in her head. Assure her that from your point of view, *less* sexual variety is compatible with *more* sexual satisfaction, although don't give up entirely on the odd fling with your feet airborne.

Q **My girlfriend – whom I haven't slept with yet – tells me she has multiple climaxes, as many as 15 in one go. I'm nervous in advance in case I don't have this effect on her.**

A If she's that orgasmic, you may find it almost impossible to sabotage her response, so please just take things in your stride.

Q My boyfriend has a huge penis – 10 inches, he says – and it hurts me during intercourse.

A This is more a problem of technique than brute size. Your boyfriend is obviously banging hard into the neck of your womb and causing quite widespread uterine pain. Changing sexual position so that your abdomen is not arched towards him will help most. Do not adopt postures where your knees begin to touch your nose. Ask him to penetrate and thrust much more gingerly than previously until you can report which angle is comfortable, then let him slowly extend his stroke.

Q **I want to experience eroticism as fully as possible. In this respect, would it be an advantage for me to be circumcised?**

A It's difficult to get a value-free judgement on this matter since all men either are or aren't circumcised, and many women *do* have a preference for 'roundheads' or 'cavaliers'. Now, if you suffer from phimosis (too-tight foreskin) or balanitis (foreskin infection) then there could be an overwhelming case in favour of the simple snip, not just to improve your sex life, but to stop the pain.

Briefly, those who are sexually pro circumcision cite improved hygiene, neatness of appearance and reduced risks of hair-trigger ejaculation. Those against largely emphasize the increased glans penis sensitivity of organs jacketed in natural skin. They also think it's time all adults learned to wash, instead of undergoing surgery out of laziness. Doctors seem to be changing their tune, however. In the US, the Academy of Pediatrics said in 1975 there were no medical benefits to be had from circumcision but it's now argued that infection of the urinary tract in baby boys is reduced by 90 per cent after circumcision so pressure to re-promote the operation is enormous. Other research has been used to suggest that partners of circumcised males also get fewer pelvic infections than those mating with 'uncut' men. Erotic verdict: not proven, decide for yourself.

Q With my first lover I once felt an incredible throbbing and yearning and wetness in my vagina which I've never been able to recapture. Is there any way I might feel those sensations again?

A This is a condition of extreme sexual arousal that can sometimes lead to a climactic syndrome called *status orgasmus*, when your response seems unlimited. You can put it down to towering young love or powerful sexual technique. Its loss may be due to the absence of either – you have possibly never felt so close to anyone since, nor in the hands of such a skilful lover.

However, you can always try to improve sensation for yourself. If you and your current boyfriend would like it, get him gently to remove all your clothes and tie your hands and feet to the bed in a safe, warm room at a quiet time of the day, fit you with a blindfold, play you arousing music, describe your beauty while bathing you from head to foot with his delicately brushing tongue, gradually moving his fingers towards your centre from the perimeter and back again, taking infinite pains and time to tingle every nerve cell connected to the surface of your skin – and when he starts to move his hand to bring you to release, he must stop, and let your excitement subside, till he's ready to begin all over again, teasing your longing till you cut the air with frustrated curses, and his fingers renew their warm progression from your perimeter to the centre, and still he waits, and still you cry, and still you are unable to find that orgasmic edge you yearn for – then, perhaps you will recapture your youthful rapture.

Q My boyfriend says he played sexual games with other boys at his private school. Does this increase the chance he will have gay affairs in future?

A Not really, because it's normal for nearly all young men and women to go through a phase of same-sex attraction around the time of puberty, whatever their future inclination. Some 10 per cent of the adult population is reportedly homosexual but you'd expect this figure to be around 70 per cent if those who had behaved like your boyfriend were entirely conditioned by these experiences.

Q My girlfriend wants me to make love to her during her period because she feels sexiest then. My mate says he caught a urethral infection from doing this with his girlfriend. Could it harm me?

A Urethral infections occur because one partner already has symptoms and transmits the problem to the other during intercourse. A woman's menstrual blood is laden with taboos but not disease (provided she is HIV-negative, of course). The days of menstrual flow coincide with a hormonal and sexual high for your girlfriend and it would be a shame to neglect her libidinal peak. If you are fussed by mess, use towels on the bed and have a post-coital wash. Better still, ask her to fit a diaphragm which not only helps with contraception, it will hold back the flow of blood that otherwise might offend your sensibility.

Q My girlfriend wants sex all the time. Is it reasonable to expect sex on demand? I'm never enthusiastic, since I'm never allowed to wait until I really want it.

A It sounds as if your woman sees you as a sexy body with very little else attached since she's obviously unaware of your persecuted feelings. In order to improve the relationship, insist she accepts a contract – on three nights a week, she can decide what happens in bed; on three nights a week, you get to choose, and Sundays are up for grabs. This way she learns that you have a choice in the matter and you get some respite. However, keep pointing out the benefits of choice over coercion, and make sure she understands that you do care for her. Part of this frantic sexual need may be simple insecurity.

Q **My boyfriend is always badgering me to have sex even when I only want a cuddle. Are men incapable of enjoying affection for its own sake?**

A No, but they need guidance. Show your man these comments from remodelled British males: 'Five minutes' naked cuddle at the end of a bad day is worth more to me than an hour's conversation.' And from a stockbroker: 'Caressing my wife, even when that's all it amounts to, reinforces our love for each other, gives me confidence that she still loves me for what I am. It is a powerful antidote to City pressures, and better than a sleeping pill.' And an ex-manual worker: 'It took a crisis for my wife and me to learn the pleasures and comfort of skin-to-skin contact. Nothing eased the pain of losing my job so much as being together in that very close but special way.'

Offer your partner this deal: suggest you spend one evening together where you get as close together as possible, removing all clothes and inhibitions, lying affectionately in each other's arms, for at least an hour, stroking and talking, even falling asleep. In return, the next night you might suggest having sex quickly and lustfully, even without fully undressing – and don't condemn it if you haven't tried it. The secret of life (and sex) is a rhythmic balance between opposites.

Q I have been going out with a delightful girl for two years but only feel like making love to her when I'm in danger of losing her. I masturbate often, have heterosexual fantasies and don't fancy men. Why am I like this?

A You have been taught by life to associate sex with anxiety. Since anxiety makes you feel uncomfortable, you tend to avoid sex rather than seek it out. However, your girlfriend is important to you so any suggestion that she's had enough of the relationship makes you feel even more anxious than you do about sex. Hence you get it on when she's about to take herself off. That's one explanation. Another would be more specific. You not only feel anxious about sex, you are angry with women for turning you on and making you want them. You are struggling for power over your own emotions and theirs. You have a deep inner need to control the dangerous forces of sexual desire and expression, perhaps because those who raised you similarly controlled their emotions or starved yours. When your woman finally says life with you is intolerable, you genuinely wish to recapture her interest and so temporary lust is regenerated. Once this purpose is served, however, libido expires. You visit on your partner the teasing, emotional withdrawal with which you were treated in infancy.

Alternatively, you simply don't fancy this woman – her skin feels wrong, she sweats too much, the sex odours are incompatible, in bed she seems gauche or louche –, but you hate the thought of losing her friendship, so you pay the price when you must. Why not try to tell her something of what you feel when you're naked together almost as an act of self-discovery? As you confront your resistances, you'll find contradictory feelings abound to give you clues. Perhaps a little therapy?

Q I've just started having sex for the first time and I love it. However, my vagina is rather sore. Is this unavoidable?

A No, the sex organs are designed to cope with considerable 'dermabrasion' from rapid and delightful thrusts. It's possible you are accepting penetration before your vagina is well lubricated, in which case we suggest you prolong the kisses of foreplay until you feel well and truly wet between the legs. If your juices still fail, try KY Jelly. But bear in mind that a good deal of genital soreness is caused by thrush. This fungal infection will always develop in warm moist areas of the body, especially if your hormone and sugar levels are high. You and your lover can also pass it back and forth, like playing ping pong, so if this is the problem make sure the doctor treats you *both*.

Q My boyfriend and I have just had our first holiday together which was blissful, but towards the end of the week I started to get this burning sensation when I went to the loo. It lasted for two or three days, then went away of its own accord. What was it?

A So-called 'honeymoon cystitis' is a result of cervical bruising, and you're lucky the pain wasn't greater. Ask your boyfriend not to crash his penis into the tip of your cervix quite so hard during sex and the problem won't recur.

Q I feel I'm going overboard sexually. I seem to be wanting it at the most unlikely times and in strange places e.g. the porch of the town hall! I'm growing scared about how easily I get carried away and my boyfriend just encourages it. I know I'll get into trouble if I'm not careful.

A Probably, unless you stop. But you don't want to stop because the experiences are violently erotic and you're hooked on them. Perhaps you seek the embarrassment (?) of public exposure to calm you down. At the same time, intense passion is a jewel in your crown and needs all the polishing you can give it. If you are really worried (rather than slightly nervous) look at your own history to see what your exhibitionism might signify. Is this a defiance of convention? A rebellion against the old school code? Are you finally shutting up all those folk who never regarded you as a sex siren? Are you compensating for former feelings of physical ugliness? Or do you really want to be caught and put away by some Puritan jury, perhaps wrapped in a scarlet letter as a woman of shame? Is it possibly your own inhibition you're displaying? And is taking an *al fresco* risk really the only way to satisfy your need?

Q We've tried to make love three times. On each occasion, my boyfriend lost his erection. Now he seems to have given up but blames me for not coming across when he knows it's inconvenient – just before an appointment, when other people are going to be around, and so on. How can I help us?

A Your lover-to-be is playing a convenient game of cover-up. Since he can't make love to you he is pretending that the true problem is that you won't make love to him. Tell him the relationship is doomed if he carries on blaming you. The truth is that you *as a couple* are having sexual difficulties. This is no one's 'fault', but simply the way things are as a product of your joint personalities. The only interesting question is, how can things be improved? Go back to basics and abandon intercourse for the time being.

Now, we assume he has no physical problems causing impaired erection, such as heart disease, hypertension, poor circulation, neurological disorders or diabetes. Second, we assume you are both full of myths about his 'responsibility' to be erect whenever you are available. Third, we guess you are both misdefining sex as penis-vagina intercourse while ignoring all the other fulfilling alternatives. Fourth, we imaging you have spent very little time getting accustomed to each other's bodies, using massage, experimenting with water, playing games,describing fantasies, teasing nipples, fooling with clothes, tickling armpits and inhaling each other's perfume (he should enjoy your sex-smell impregnated on silk; you should enjoy his fresh on the hair of his armpit).

Once you have become relaxed and happy in each other's naked company, having learned to talk and play with anxiety, you can offer mutual orgasm by hand. Maybe you'd like to add a game to this as well. Some people like mild smacks on the buttocks first. Others pretend to be virgins all over again. Still others tie their lover's thumbs together before anointing and caressing the genitals. The most determined sybarites makes sure their partners get masturbated as *slowly* as possible, thereby intensifying sensations to a mountainous degree. The effect of all this is to prevent anyone from worrying about their response because they are so intent on obtaining gratification.

Failing conventional masturbation, the *Paradis Charnels* (1903) mentions nine sites on the human body for alternative sex — mouth, breasts, armpit, fingers (locked into a hollow), knee, elbow, hair rolled into a loop or into a lasso-shape, and anus (though check your local laws, use condoms, be gentle, and wash afterwards). Having got this far, we believe your boyfriend will have learned that erections automatically occur when he gets close to someone he finds attractive, who doesn't make him feel anxious and who wishes to make love to him as a person.

Q When we were both virgins, we vowed we would love one another for life. Apart from being mad about each other, it meant we'd never get AIDS from sex. We're both 19, have been going to bed for just over a year and the sex is a disaster. I come too quickly or she takes too long. I feel very guilty but cannot see how I'm going to survive like this for the rest of my life.

A Your romantic principles do you credit but they've just been shipwrecked by reality. It may be possible for a sex therapist to help you improve your joint erotic timing but we question whether that would solve all your mutual emotional problems. The marriage-promise to love someone for life is hard to keep under any circumstances. Late teens is a time of turmoil when you truly feel like establishing a few guidelines, for example a personal 60-year plan, and yet the feeling of insecurity passes and then the plans can read like prison sentences. Early marital commitments are those most likely to end in divorce, in a relatively short space of time, for one overwhelming reason. You may have finished growing, but you haven't yet finished growing aware. It would indeed be wonderful if you could continue loving each other passionately for all the days of your generation but possibly the disillusionment about sex is the first sign of a process of re-evaluation.

Q **My husband sits downstairs watching TV till
one in the morning, long after I am asleep,
and then wakes me up to make love. I hate
refusing in case he thinks I no longer care for
him but I have to work and can't afford to
miss my rest.**

A Well, don't try to reform him in the middle of the
night. When you are both relaxed, perhaps after
dinner, get him to reschedule sex or bedtime.
Point out that this is in his own best interest
because you are putting your foot down. Explain,
for example, that there's nothing to stop him
joining you in bed around ten for a lovely slow
'Viennese oyster', 'Pompoir' or 'English rocking-
chair' (if he's slow on the uptake, refer him to *The
Joy Of Sex*) since you don't mind if he gets up
later to watch old films till breakfast.

Q **My husband had a rotten family life himself
and I can see he married me to make up for
that. But he feels very easily rejected and I'm
caught in a dilemma. I want to cut down
some of our lovemaking because it becomes
meaningless to me but I know he'll be upset.
How can I manage it?**

A By using the 'scratched record' technique to tell
him repetitively that you do love and wish to be
with him but you positively need less frequent
sex in order to improve the remainder. Support
this position by giving him extra hugs, cuddles
and declarations of love. It won't be easy at first,
because he obviously regards sex as the principal
proof of love, but if you can get him to see you
feel even closer than before, he might possibly
feel grateful that some of the performance
pressure has been removed.

Q It's very simple. My boyfriend is just no good in bed. He comes too quickly and doesn't have a clue about how to stimulate me. Is there any point in telling him? I'm losing heart but I'm reluctant to become promiscuous.

A Sounds to us as though you've given up. Maybe you're right. Maybe you've explored the squeeze technique for premature ejaculation (see page 18). Maybe you've shown him in exact detail how you stimulate yourself and would wish him to copy. And possibly he still hasn't got a hope of making you happy. Perhaps, though, there might be a friendship instead? It is possible to stay mates with an old lover sometimes to the point where that relationship outlasts other, full-blooded love affairs. However, maybe you also have trouble with 'endings', in deciding that it really is time you moved along. (Incidentally, having a replacement love affair could hardly be termed 'promiscuity', i.e. 'indiscriminate sexual intercourse').

Q My man is a 'dream lover'. He pays court to me, buys me flowers, takes me to dinner, kisses me passionately, is always in raptures about me and implies we'd positively sizzle together in bed. Only trouble is, he never takes me there and we've never made love. Why not?

A You're not getting any voluntary explanations so if you want one you'd better ask him. He could have a wife. He may fear AIDS. He might be impotent (strong possibility, we think). He may have a sexually-transmitted disease. He may possess spiritual beliefs which preclude intercourse. He may have a psychological fear of the vagina. He may be saving himself for the woman he intends to marry, which might still be you. Whatever it is, we guess the relationship won't develop until you two talk turkey.

Q My girlfriend uses the dangers of AIDS as a means of trying to prevent me having relationships with other women. I admit I'm a flirt but she and I have always had an excellent love life and till now I haven't ever wanted anyone else, but I swear she's putting the idea into my head.

A Your girlfriend's fear of being abandoned seems to interlock with your fear of being found undesirable and that insecurity is what you two have in common. Unfortunately, you are each trying to compel the other to resolve your emotional problems. She is now telling you to have no women friends at all, which is her way of using power to feel safe, and you are telling her you may have to start another relationship soon, which is your way of forcing her to confess she can't live without you.

The only means of limiting the destructive impact of these psychological games is to become aware of them. Persuade her to discuss her past experience of rejection, including this anxiety that AIDS might be the final nail in her coffin, and also any times when sex has let her down. Have many men, especially her father, proved unloving? And since you flirt so often, can you not offer an insight into this behaviour? Your background must include relevant teenage times when you felt unattractive, full of shyness and acne, or perhaps lonely and isolated? If she could understand your anxieties she could begin to make some allowance for your actions. Possibly the relief of soul-baring would help you avoid being unfaithful. Taking responsibility for your *own* respective vulnerabilities is the only way forward because if you two don't open up, we can't help believing you're going to break up.

Q My boyfriend has got hold of one of those old-fashioned books from the 1970s and is urging me to combine Chinese philosophy with our love life. I've always been common-sensical about sex and just cannot get into tantric yoga after a busy week in the office. How can anyone take that stuff seriously?

A What's more to the point, your boyfriend is taking it seriously. You know him better than we do. Does this mean he's having another fad? Or could he be asking for a slightly more spiritual relationship? Instead of asserting what you can't believe in (because no one can change that unless you let them), ask yourself this question. Is your partnership simply convenient, short on meaning, or does it have a solid future? If you could get to the bottom of this together, one of two things would follow. Either you'd feel closer and more tolerant, or it would become clear that you have little in common. This might be painful enlightenment, but you'd know where you stand.

Q I woke up last night and realized that my wife, lying in bed beside me, was masturbating. I didn't say anything but I am upset. It's not that I think there's something wrong with masturbation. I don't. But we had made love that night already. Am I not enough for her?

A Obviously, you feel sad about this and believe somehow you are sexually insufficient. But we question whether *her* behaviour does really need to be seen as a reflection on *yours?* Assuming your wife has a climax during intercourse, there could be several reasons why later in the night she wants another, yet it would be most inconsiderate to waken you from sleep. She could be more highly sexed than you realize, or have become so. She could be going through a phase when life is generally very stimulating, and remember that any stimulation is convertible to sexuality. She could be waking up full of simple tension which can most easily be relieved by orgasm, a means of relaxation preferred to pills or alcohol. She could be at a phase of her menstrual cycle producing maximum libido. And should she be pregnant, her body could be in a near-permanent state of arousal for that reason alone.

In these circumstances, why should she use you as a casual relief of 'additional' sexual feelings which are everything to do with her and nothing to do with you? Or are you really saying you should be in control of her entire sexual 'output'? By all means, enquire whether she would like to vary the sexual pattern between you. But do try to see the wider possibilities.

Q My husband masturbates a lot. I accepted this to begin with, but lately we've had much less sex together and I'm resenting it furiously. Why, when he's got me there, does he need to wank?

A This is a different problem from the one just discussed, precisely because the sexual relationship here is deteriorating. Naturally, your husband's masturbation could still represent a form of comfort and relaxation, even therapy. But from your point of view, he also seems to be using it as escape, withdrawal and punishment. You have to ask yourself: why might he be angry with me? Or why is he afraid to make love any more? Or have his feelings declined? Or just what 'unfinished business' is there between us? We don't think there's any point in complaining to others without talking to him.

Q My woman friend told me that she and her husband are happy to lie next to each other in bed masturbating. When I told my husband and suggested *we* should try, he laughed and said that was for people who had sex problems. I can see there's more to it than that and really looked forward to something new. Now I feel stuck in my sexual relationship and am really upset.

A It sounds as though your marriage is making you restless in contrast to your husband who is very settled. If he's content sexually, then your request, coming out of the literal blue, may indeed seem comic, but this is missing the 'hidden agenda' behind it. 'Somehow', you are saying, 'I want to feel more stimulated by us, not only sexually, but emotionally'. It would be helpful if you could try and tell him about the *other* changes you would like to make in your life together. It sounds as though you want to do something 'unconventional' or 'unexpected' before middle age saps your spirit. If you took him parachute jumping, for example, who knows what leaps of the imagination he'd be able to make.

Q I have a secret I'd love to tell my wife but daren't. I adore anal sex. She is far too innocent to understand but I feel starved and fear the consequences.

A This is understandable only if you know your wife to be a total prude with rectal phobia. Otherwise, you are making the classic mistake of being unable to see your wife as a whole person. Innocent she may be but that doesn't mean she wouldn't entertain any number of spontaneously proposed sexual variations. It all depends how you make her feel. And if you have had much more sexual experience than she has and feel guilty about it, open up your feelings of guilt. It is only when you give her the chance to know and accept the real you *and if you can do the same for her* that your marriage will develop and become rewarding. It's even possible she'll go further, playing Doctors and Nurses, offering that special prostatic massage (use KY Jelly and rubber gloves) which drives most men wild! We should not have to add that anal intercourse is illegal in many parts of the Anglo-Saxon world and that seeking casual, extra-marital anal sex not only increases the risk of you getting HIV but of your wife doing so too.

Q **My husband is one of the ugliest men I have ever met but I'm totally turned on by him. He is enormously attractive to me. My friends and parents say I must be kinky but if anything marriage has encouraged the attraction. I can't get enough of him. He is very loving in return. But am I perverted?**

A What is perversion, indeed what is beauty? About 97 per cent of the population fail to meet 'ideals' in both regards. The ideals are based on anxiety – 'Don't take risks'; 'Pretty people are safest' – and themselves are questionable, since pillars of society have been known to crumble and beautiful folk are frequently narcissistically cruel. However, you can't have a whole relationship with somebody's face, pretty or otherwise, and that applies in your case too. Maybe you are using your relationship to make unconscious statements, like 'Look! I'm Saint Beauty who rescued the Beast!', or 'I'll show you how to declare independence!', to family and friends. If face value is the basis of your marriage, rather than just a cue for arousal, the union will fail when the audience grows bored. But we think there's hope in your realization that 'he is very loving in return', implying you place value on feelings as well as faces.

Q My husband works in a night club but I've never bothered about the fact he's surrounded by strippers and hostesses. We've always been crazy about each other. When I thought I might be pregnant (I'm not though) he stopped making love to me and brought home some pornographic books which he read in bed. It was as if he were saying 'You mustn't change your shape or appearance, otherwise I won't fancy you'. Am I reading too much into this?

A We believe in trusting to instinct in situations like this and if that's what struck you, it's possibly correct. He works in a milieu where women are valued for youth and beauty. There may be many interesting reasons why he wants his wife to remain young and attractive but none of them hide the fact that this is partly rejecting and unrealistic. One day, baby or not, you are going to age, just as he is. How could you fail to feel insecure about him? Try to get him to 'see the message' he was so clearly giving you and ask him to consider the basis of his attitude. Will he ever wish to be a father? Or is he eventually going to 'fire' you, as he'd fire a club hostess, when you get the wrong side of 35? Your relationship seems actually rockier than you realize.

Q My wife found a girlie book recently at the office and she brought it home. We got very aroused and made fantastic love. Afterwards, I realized she'd been turned on by some of the lesbian photos. What could this mean?

A For 99.9 per cent of the population, fantasy and reality are distinct. Clearly, your wife likes the idea of 'imagining' lesbian sex scenes, or at least she has done so for about half an hour, but that doesn't prove anything further. Homosexuals are perfectly capable of getting excited by imagining 'straights' in bed, but wouldn't want one for Christmas.

Q We make amazing love together but my husband never says 'I love you' – not once. I'm all over him just after we've had sex but I feel he withholds from me on purpose.

A People who find it difficult to express love have rarely heard professions of love in their own original families. This failure to verbalize affection becomes a tradition, therefore, a 'part of the way WE behave'. Parents who can't speak love often cannot communicate love physically either. So your husband is conceivably backward in offering cuddles too. This means the sex act probably has to work overtime in representing the total emotional expression of which he is currently capable. See, therefore, whether he won't open up a bit verbally *during* sex. Some men hate it when sex is 'interrupted' by conversation. But others learn to love talking, even talking 'dirty', joking, sharing moods, describing fantasies or revealing anxious feelings at a time when their confidence is greatest because their bodies are relished.

Q My husband follows me all over the house stroking me as if I were a cat. I liked this at the beginning of our relationship and it would often turn into wonderful sex. Now it's driving me mad with irritation. We can't have sex all the time!

A In fact, most people don't stroke cats in order to have sex with them but because they need to make calm, affectionate contact with the world outside themselves. You seem to feel your husband's only intention is bedwards. Yet it's also possible his petting is saying 'I think you look/feel/are terrific', without further hidden purpose. Significantly, the idea of extra sex with him makes you equally angry, so we have to notice that the relationship may have other strains besides the weight of his fingers on your hair or flank. You sound very busy. Perhaps the real issue is workshare? If he does tend to overdo it sexwise and under-contribute otherwise, hand over some of the tasks you are so burdened by. If he shared household responsibility he would have less time to be demanding and you would have more time in which to feel desirous.

Q My girlfriend has parents who never gave her any privacy. Her mother would even follow her into the bathroom and she was forbidden to lock the door. From time to time, she is very reclusive to the point of shutting me out of her life, so we row. Then she sulks and won't make love for a week.

A Your girlfriend needs some personal help to see that she is periodically treating you as an intrusive parent while failing to act as a caring partner herself. Try to point her in the direction of some professional counselling while reiterating that you do understand her dilemma and its background, and you're not going to run away.

Q My boyfriend is pathologically jealous of every man I meet at work, at home or in the street. He says I am having affairs everywhere when I'm only trying to have one with him. He gets moody and violent, then says if I try to leave he'll kill us both.

A This worrying behaviour seems exceptionally bewildering, since you have done none of the things he accuses you of, yet the dynamics of it are only too familiar to psychotherapists. You are like a cinema screen onto which he has projected all his feelings of insecurity and self-doubt. These will be considerable and entirely pre-date your association. History has only taught him to regard intimacy as betrayal. Relatives or past guardians have proved seriously unreliable. Like anyone else, he genuinely wishes to get close to others, but when this is achieved, he is overcome by remembered waves of apprehension and anger. His only defence is to accuse you of infidelity. If he doesn't attack, then he has to face overwhelming pain instead. He is afraid to believe you could love him in case he recalls his deprivation. If instead you are perceived to be 'just like all the rest', he can continue to pretend that love itself is a myth.

In this predicament, it's perfectly natural for the human mind to prefer irrational thoughts to reality. Yet he urgently needs help, just as you need to avoid becoming his victim. When he makes these accusations, don't attempt denials because they only feed his fantasies. Try to get him to say what he feels; to talk about his experience of unhappiness, switching the conversation towards the benefits of discussing this with a professional counsellor. It won't be easy, but you also need to think hard about your escape plan, even your moonlight flit, however much you thereby confirm his pessimistic suspicion.

Q My girlfriend is a great lover but she says she can never make the first move in bed. We've talked our heads off about this without making any progress.

A Talking isn't enough. She needs to put in some action. A good way to begin is by undertaking mutual massage. Prepare the time, place and circumstances (warm room; baby oil; soft music; candlelight). Take turns, 20 minutes each, to pleasure the other with small, circling strokes on the back and shoulders, slowing the movements down to create maximum impact. This will teach your partner to become sensually *active* without making her too self-conscious. In the first few sessions, give each other feedback to say which strokes are nicest. By session three, include the remainder of the body. Avoid intercourse altogether until at least session five, if you can last that long, and even then defer it if you'd rather. By session six or seven, when she is massaging you, and when she's clearly got you to a point of powerful erotic response, draw attention to her achievement and suggest she uses her own judgement over the next few minutes about taking matters further, ideally in the woman-on-top position. This may seem like a roundabout solution to your problem but it does protect her anxieties and it will be fun.

Q I recently began a successful flat-share with another man, my best friend. However, the other night he told me he was gay, he loved me and wanted me. I'm stunned. Should I leave?

A Why should you give up house and home because a person has made a pass at you? Your options remain the same. You can say, 'Yes, I'm interested', 'No, I'm not interested', or remain undecided. You can do exactly what you would have done had your friend been a woman making the same advances. Walking out is a way of avoiding difficult feelings, not dealing with them. Possibly, you're embarrassed, but there is life after embarrassment. By staying, you also allow your friend to sort out his feelings about love, sex and friendship too. Maybe he will have to learn to live with your 'No'. But if you run away, you only teach him to feel uncomfortable about himself.

Q I'm very confused. I've always needed to make love to my boyfriend often. Each time he said he didn't want to marry me, I'd desire him more (I know this sounds kinky) But now he appears to be ready for marriage and I'm beginning to go off him sexually. I'm scared I'll end up his wife but with no sex drive. What's happening to me?

A His past attitude towards marriage seems to have undermined your confidence. In order to compensate, you initiated a lot of sex. Now that he has offered you commitment, your anxiety is subsiding. As a result, you can get a more realistic picture of how often you wish to make love, which may be less than you formerly realized.

There is another explanation, however, which concerns your anger. Now that you feel less worried, you are probably able, for the first time, to feel angry with him for all those rejections. If you can say how hurt you felt and he can take it you'll be fine. If he can't cope, try at least expressing it to someone reliable and friendly whom you know to be a good listener. It's also valuable to take a wider look at his past reasons for not wanting to marry. You are seeing these only in personal terms but isn't it possible that his reluctance had as much to do with worries over his age, financial position, and even a general fear of being trapped, as with you directly? Understanding this will allow you to feel much better about yourself as a woman *and* a lover.

2 The sex life of parents

Q **My husband thinks his penis will hurt our unborn baby during intercourse.**

A It isn't possible. Sex is perfectly safe from this point of view until towards the very end of a *normal* pregnancy, right up to the baby's expected date of birth, although if your husband is a heavy man he should avoid lying across your stomach. Perhaps unconsciously what your husband really fears is that the baby will damage his penis, rather than the other way round. Many men have the fantasy that the baby will bite them during intercourse. It hasn't happened yet!

Q **Should my wife avoid having orgasms for fear they will damage our baby?**

A Provided the pregnancy is normal, there is absolutely nothing to indicate that orgasm will hurt or threaten your unborn child. It is even possible that orgasm rehearses the uterus for the eventual contractions of birth, thus making labour shorter and easier. The chemicals released by sexual pleasure may also affect the situation of the foetus beneficially. (It cannot hurt to feel contentment at second-hand.) The only time when orgasm should be avoided is in the case of threatened miscarriage. Here the doctor will advise abstention from sex at around the third month of the pregnancy. You will be told if sex may be resumed before the birth.

Q I've just found out my husband was unfaithful to me throughout my first pregnancy. I am devastated. He says he doesn't understand why he did it.

A He probably doesn't, but this is not to make excuses and 'understanding' by itself is not going to prevent you feeling betrayed. The situation is very common because men so often feel threatened by the implications of the pregnancy. First, they may be dismayed by the physical changes of pregnancy itself. Deep inside, some men feel 'cheated' by the loss of the sexy body they married. Second, they may dislike the focus of attention shifting to you and your dominant role in reproduction. Third, they may feel frightened of 'sharing' you with the new baby. Fourth, they can easily get depressed thinking about the cost of an extra mouth to feed, as well as the responsibility of fatherhood. In general, men function by seeking rapid gratification of their ego-wishes. They find it hard to endure months of domestic drama without a 'starring' role. Hence their frequent bad behaviour. You have to try to pick up the pieces as you find them on the floor. Don't pretend; vent your feelings and see whether you can both learn from the hurt and sorrow.

Q As I get more pregnant, our favourite sex positions become impossible.

A Try the 'scissors' position during mid-pregnancy since it allows the man to take some of his weight off his partner. Instead of placing his legs between hers, or one on either side, he puts one between and one outside – hence the scissors effect. In later pregnancy, only rear entry, side-by-side or seated postures are feasible but one of you will have to pleasure your clitoris by hand.

Q **I have just had thrush and trichomoniasis. Could these infections hurt my baby?**

A No, the baby is protected by the placenta. Thrush is common during pregnancy because of your raised hormone levels, so ensure you wear cotton underwear, and go easy on the sugar intake since it's food for the fungus.

Q **Is my wife peculiar because she is ten times randier now than she was before getting pregnant?**

A Contrary to myth, pregnant women get *more* not less interested in sex because sexual tension is actually produced in the body at this time. Your wife is obviously making the most of it. We hope you are as well.

Q **My husband has had non-specific urethritis in the past. Should we avoid sex until after the birth?**

A If he was successfully treated, there is nothing to worry about. If he still has the infection, you might contract it and your baby might be born with 'sticky eye', although this can also be treated. Other sexual conditions which might affect the unborn and newborn child include syphilis, cytomegalovirus, herpes, gonorrhoea and of course HIV. Each poses special risks to the baby and to you, threatening life or future fertility. If you have any worries, talk to your doctor.

Q My woman is always too tired for sex now she's pregnant. How long is this going to go on?

A The commonest pattern is for her to feel tired and under the weather for the first three months; full of energy and sexual interest in the middle three months; then heavier and less interested in the last three months. In extreme cases, you may find she doesn't want to know for a full *nine* months. But since fatigue would be the key cause, part of the remedy is up to you. The more you help in the kitchen, the greater your chance in the bedroom.

Q Morning sickness all day and all night is crippling my love life. Will it ever stop?

A It usually ends around the 13th to 15th week of pregnancy, though some unfortunates carry on vomiting for the entire nine months, often because they're carrying twins. Acupressure bands worn on the wrists are believed to alleviate the complaint. You can ask at your pharmacy for details. They are quite harmless.

Q My husband says he can't make love to me because I'm pregnant. I've got months to go. What *are* we going to do?

A If he loves you but has pregnancy hang-ups, encourage him into lots of loving non-vaginal sex (for a brief guide, see page 146). You can obviously enjoy the benefit of relaxing mutual massage which is good for him, you *and* the baby. If the relationship itself has been in distress for a while, be aware that his refusal may contain a hostile or rejecting message. Although it's a terrible time to face the possibility, you may have to consider the degree of his commitment and fidelity.

Q Now that I'm heavily pregnant, I crave my husband physically and emotionally but cannot climax. Why am I being robbed?

A Sexual congestion and tension is so extreme during the final month before the birth that often orgasm cannot relieve the burden. Paradoxically, you may experience a 'milder' orgasm than normal, or even no orgasm at all. Extreme exhaustion may also impair your ability to respond to your own sources of arousal, whether during intercourse or masturbation. It is one of the extra prices you pay for the pleasures of motherhood.

Q Can masturbation damage my unborn child?

A Not at all. However, should it be your custom, do not insert any sharp or over-solid object inside your vagina (that includes vibrators).

Q I'm worried I'll never want sex again because of my pregnancy. I reassure my husband, but can *you* reassure *me?*

A After the birth, interest in sex tends to return slowly. Continued breast-feeding will delay desire by keeping prolactin levels high but libido tends to trickle back after about three months. If after six months you still feel sexless, then it would be worth consulting your doctor. However, your *current* problem is *anxiety*, and that's also a condition made worse by pregnancy and changing hormone levels.

Q **Will I lose my libido once pregnancy is over? I worry about it 'going back to normal' since for me that means little interest and sporadic orgasms.**

A It doesn't have to, provided you decide that in future you will focus on your sexual needs rather than simply 'putting up with things'. We hope the rest of this book will provide the answers to your problems.

Q **Are some men specially attracted to pregnant women?**

A It's possible for men to be very excited by pregnancy, in general or in particular, but rare in our experience for a husband to go 'overboard' only in the nine months prior to the birth. Equally rare is the 'pregnancy fetishist'. Some men try to have sex with women pregnant by others in the hope of exploiting a vulnerable situation. More common still is the woman-hater who feels hostile to all potential mothers.

Q **I've had very romantic extra-marital affairs during all my three pregnancies but went off the men as soon as I gave birth. Why should I behave so bizarrely?**

A 'Pregnancy sexuality' may have driven you into other men's arms, a combination of physical arousal and emotional abandon. Perhaps you almost felt drunk with the excitement of creating life? Your own husband's indifference at these special times may have contributed. The reversal of these feelings, plus fatigue, would account for going off the men afterwards.

Q **My friend says she had her first orgasm because she was pregnant. Could this be true?**

A Yes. The hormonal changes in her body may have 'surprised' her into heightened responses, including first orgasm. Some women compare giving birth to orgasm. Others obtain the same pleasure from breast-feeding.

Q **My orgasm seems to have moved its position now I'm seven months pregnant.**

A Yes, the area of your womb in which it is possible for you to detect orgasmic contractions has been expanded by late pregnancy, hence the new locus of sensation.

Q **My sister told me she had an orgasm when she gave birth. I *hated* giving birth and I just can't believe it.**

A Women seem to have enormously varied experiences of childbirth, from heaven to hell. The picture is distorted by those writers who generalize from their own ecstatic or diabolic confinements. One woman was told by a French gynaecologist – 'Madame, you gave birth like a flower' – a picturesque simile. Others find the path distinctly thorny. Still others, generally those carrying smaller babies, discover that not only is birth painless but the contractions are sexually stimulating. The literally crowning experience, as the baby's head pushes its way through the birth canal across the clitoris, is that of climax. Your sister is probably telling the truth.

Q **Can the experience of childbirth impair my orgasmic abilities?**

A Unless childbirth has necessitated major surgery on your vagina and uterus, your ability to enjoy sex to orgasm should remain the same.

Q **I've had a episiotomy and now sex is agony. What have the doctors done to me?**

A Perhaps not quite their best. In most cases, the site of an episiotomy heals like any other wound or cut. Once the area feels comfortable, so too will intercourse. At first, you can expect soreness but this should have passed by six weeks after the birth. If it has not, then the odds are that you have been poorly sutured, creating a largish area of scar tissue. This can turn intercourse into slow torture, as you will have discovered. Without further attention, the problem will probably disappear after some six months but martyrdom has little to recommend it. Tell your doctor what's gone wrong and ask if you can be restitched.

Q How soon is it safe to have sex after childbirth?

A Depends what you mean by safe. Some hospitals advise you to abstain from intercourse for six weeks but most people find this excessive. In France, the medical advice is three weeks. The reason for abstaining at all is to avoid the danger of uterine infection while the lining of the womb is still healing. The drying up of the lochia (maternal blood) is the signal that this is complete, a process varying from woman to woman. For some, the blood loss may end after 10 days. For others, it may continue for all of six weeks. The idea of safety also includes the risk or possibility of pregnancy. Some misguidedly believe you can't conceive immediately after childbirth, but there are many '10-month babies' to prove them wrong.

Q How soon after childbirth will I feel like having sex again?

A Most mothers go through a sexual lull after giving birth, partly because the routine of caring for a new-born child is exhausting and partly because there are major fluctuations in various mood-altering hormones at this time. However, the fact that your sexual desire may be on the temporary wane does not mean you won't have strong feelings of love for your partner. Indeed, many women feel so passionate and tender at this stage of their life that they want to translate it into sex almost regardless of desire. So the answer to your question depends on your personality and on the state of your relationship with your partner. If after four or five months you still get no real pleasure out of sex then your situation deserves professional help.

Q My husband and I have always had a happy love life but with the arrival of baby we are getting self-conscious. How *can* you make love with a baby in the next room?

A New parenthood is obviously weighing you down. The enormous responsibility of having a baby can often work as a major passion-killer, especially in the first few months after the birth. Sometimes, you just need to pace yourself till you can believe the baby won't expire just because you close the door for half an hour (assuming of course that it is physically normal, warm, cosy and sleeping). But if its presence seems too onerous, there's no objection to parking baby in the pram in the spare room or bathroom while you relax into sexual reunion.

Q Our new baby sleeps in our bedroom and goes for hours without waking up. I love her being so close to me at night and it's convenient for breast-feeding, but I am worried she might be adversely affected by hearing us make love.

A Despite the views of psychoanalyst Melanie Klein, very few people can remember much of their infancy before the age of two, certainly not without prompting. Even if your child did turn out to have total recall, she wouldn't necessarily interpret your lovemaking noises as fearsome or distressing. It's even possible she may derive comfort from the routine and regular 'cries and murmurs' of love and delight surrounding her bed. Alternatively, she may regard them as 'aural wallpaper' or background static. We're sure you don't worry in the same way in case she hears you snore or sneeze, so isn't anxiety singling out your sexual activity for unfair concern? Bear in mind that some children can sleep through any kind of noise, especially in the first deep-sleep hours of the night.

Q My wife's vagina seems too loose for sex since the birth of our second child. I told her this and she got very cross and hurt. But could I be right?

A You might well be right but she could still feel distressed. How are you going to take care of *both* eventualities? Let's suppose her vagina has been 're-shaped' by the travail of childbirth. She did not wish this to happen; it's just one more circumstance to which she as a human being must adapt. The physical problem can easily be solved by suggesting sex positions which keep her legs together ('male missionary'; rear or side entry etc). You might also encourage her to do her Kegel exercises which flex the pubococcygeal muscles, the muscles controlling urination, to tone up her 'pelvic floor'. These can be practised at any time of day but especially when going to the bathroom. Explain that she should stop her urinary stream in mid-flow, count to three, re-start the flow, count to three, stop, re-start, and so on till the bladder seems empty, repeating up to thrice daily. On other occasions, the PC muscles can be exercised at will – walking, sitting, travelling.

Some women eventually manage to 'body-build' in this zone until they can actually grip and milk the penis during sex without the need for further bodily movement but for the time being, restoring muscle tone is the target. The emotional problem needs a different approach. Why not make it clear you had absolutely no intention of making her feel like a freak? You could even apologize if you consider you expressed yourself clumsily.

Q Our toddler climbed on my husband's back (fortunately my husband was under the bedclothes) because he thought daddy was playing a 'horsey' game when he was actually having intercourse with me. Could he be troubled by this experience?

A We think it's more likely to have 'damaged' you than the child, especially in relation to enjoying a relaxed orgasm or two. Your toddler had no reason to think this was anything other than another 'horsey' game with Dad. You're the one who got the shock of your life. (It probably didn't do much for Dad's concentration either.)

Q My wife's vagina seems too tight for sex since the birth of our second child. I get the feeling she is trying to 'shut me out', although she insists this is not true.

A If your wife had any surgical intervention at the birth, she may have been stitched up inexpertly, thus creating your problem. Simple explanations that fit the facts should always be explored first, so ask your wife to get a check-up. Failing a physical explanation for your wife's tightness, then she may indeed be too tense to allow easy sexual penetration. What's the chance of you *consciously* trying to alleviate some of the daily pressures in her life (work, children, home) to find out whether a refreshed partner is a more sexually welcoming one? Increasing your cuddling rate might also assist. We don't think your wife has 'vaginismus' (full-scale, involuntary muscle spasm of the genitals). We feel the problem is likely to have resulted from more ordinary stresses.

Q **I am deeply embarrassed by breast-feeding since it turns me on sexually.**

A Well, then you'd better learn to do something with your extra sexuality, such as inform your partner of your (temporarily) increased needs, or even take matters into your own hands from time to time during the day. It would be a shame to give up the benefits of breast-feeding simply because you couldn't accept the odd extra orgasm, wouldn't it?

Q **I had lovely big boobs when I breast-fed. Now they look as if they've been sucked dry. It isn't fair and my husband keeps making uncomplimentary comments.**

A Life is not fair, and nor is your husband. The only radical remedy is cosmetic 'augmentation' but it's expensive, carries an operational risk and the results cannot be guaranteed. We question anyway whether it's essential. Your husband is really complaining about one of the *facts* of human ageing. That's his problem and there is no call for you to make it yours. Tell him how his remarks make you feel (depressed, grumpy, unsexy, put-down) and get him to explore what his complaints show he wants (more visual stimulation, more cuddling and mothering, more youthful sauciness; in a word more titillation). Your *joint* needs can be compensated for by changing behaviour in bed rather than the surgeon's knife.

Q When we make love, the moment I get
aroused my breasts leak – and I'll be breast-
feeding for another 12 months! Help!

A It it's mess that puts you off, use towels in bed
and dispense with night clothes. If, on the other
hand, you are beginning to feel that babies and
sexuality are getting uncomfortably associated,
perhaps even incestuously, then don't keep this
distress to yourself. Confide in your partner so he
can say 'I can cope for the short time it takes for
this breast-reflex to die down and I'll do my best
to help you feel that way too'. Show him this
answer. Breast leakage mainly happens in the first
days of breast-feeding. Later, when feeds are fewer,
it won't occur – so hang in there.

Q My husband and I have always enjoyed him
caressing my breasts during sex but at present
they are too painful to touch. The problem is
we just don't know how to get started any
more – we've lost our starting point.

A Lovemaking routines are *not* the bad idea so-
called sexperts used to suggest. Many couples
establish a delightful pattern of which they rarely
tire and some evidence shows lovers to stick to
the same pattern over 20, 30 and 40 years of bliss.
However, you are compelled, for the time being,
to suspend yours so make a deliberate search for
alternative mood-making sites (such as the sense-
rich declivities of the side of the neck, where the
odd lovebite might provide a satisfactory arousal
trigger, or well-washed toes which you can suck
with beguiling consequences).

Q It's four months since the birth of our first child but my wife still has a 'take it or leave it' approach to sex. She can always get up to breast-feed the child so why can't she look after me?

A She is not your mother, although you sound as though you want one. Your child has an absolute requirement to be fed. Your wife is quite right to consider this a priority. Young parenthood is a phase of life when many of your emotional needs have to take second place. Somehow, you cannot reach that adult perspective but have got lost in your sulky inner child. Maybe your wife is picking up on this. It could be she needs another adult in her life at present and so finds it hard to relate to a 'second child'. Consider, therefore, whether there are reasons for your reactions which are *all to do with yourself.* Is it true that you have often felt displaced by others (brothers and sisters in childhood, perhaps?). Or were you raised by your family to believe you always had to be put first in the pecking list (and therefore get anxious when required to wait)?

Try to find a way to explain some of this to your partner, as well as to yourself, so she can see you are striving to understand and change. If she has problems of her own, try to work through them with this checklist:

- Is she anxious about about a further pregnancy? What have you done about birth control?
- Has she unpleasant memories of her recent labour? If it was long and traumatic, she may associate scx with pain. Your wife may be reassured to know that most women find a second labour easier than the first, supposing they are young and healthy.
- Is she angry or depressed? Has anyone's behaviour, during or after the pregnancy, helped to turn her off? Do these feelings have a traceable

pedigree? Is she brought low by the thought that
'history is repeating itself'? Get her to say what's
on her mind.

● If nothing seems to account for the problem,
ask the doctor to arrange a hormone test.
Sometimes these chemical messengers go haywire
after pregnancy with loss of sexual desire as an
unwanted effect.

Q **We've only been married nine months and
already I've had an abortion because my
husband insisted we couldn't afford to start a
family. He's forgotten all about it, but I can't
bear him to touch me.**

A It's probable that you are grieving for the baby you
were not able to have. You must have pictured
your child in your mind, thinking how it would
alter your life. It sounds as if you also wanted this
baby despite any impracticalities. Your husband
did not make the same mental pictures and so he
does not have the same emotions, but this does
not imply he cannot be made to understand
yours. You may be angry with him at several
levels. Yes, he was quick to insist the pregnancy
must end. Possibly he was careless earlier about
birth control. However, conception does take two
and you may have been reckless about taking
precautions as well. Try to convey what it has all
meant for you so he can begin to accept your
distress. If you could feel that he were more
sympathetic, shouldering his share of the guilt,
you would be able to reconstruct your sexual
relationship.

Q **In the months following the birth of our child, my man seems to have deserted us. He's always too busy to spend time at home. He insists nothing is wrong, and wants sex much more than before but I now find it hard to respond.**

A We guess part of you feels cross with him for his absences and that's the bit that doesn't want to gratify him sexually. After all, he seems to be taking his family for granted and 'treating his home like an hotel'. If your sex life is going to improve, then your emotional conflicts have first to be resolved. Men often cope poorly with the arrival of a new child, feeling severely displaced. They tend to carve out blocks of 'quality' personal time by themselves as a compensation. On the assumption that you have given up paid work for a while, your husband may also feel under strong pressure financially. Even his increased sex drive can be interpreted as a sign of anxiety rather than passion. So tackle him. Explain that you feel lonely and bereft and say that you've wondered whether he's entirely happy . . .

Q My husband hasn't touched me since our child was born. Previously, he couldn't get enough lovemaking. Is this how men are?

A A common feeling for men after the first baby arrives is that life has stopped being fun. Instead, it has become full of heavy responsibilities. This can seem truly depressing and the lack of sex may be a reflection of that sense of depression. Maybe becoming a parent has distorted his view of both of you? And possibly for the first time, he identifies himself with his father, you with his mother, which would certainly distort his sense of desire. Very soon, you will have to take him away for a weekend, having parked baby with *your* mother, and help him confront the feelings behind his sexual denial. Perhaps he's irrationally angry with you for changing a 'happy two' into a 'burdensome three'? If so, he still has to put this into words and work through the rage. It would be in your interests to let him express this hostility even though you can imagine more attractive uses for your spare time.

Q We had a sex problem before the birth of our baby. I was told there was no point in attempting sex therapy until the pregnancy was over. Is this right?

A Yes, you wouldn't have been able to carry out the 'homework' massages properly, and your hormone levels would not have been 'normal', so it was best to wait until now.

Q I can't make love to my wife unless I fantasize she is a young prostitute instead of a young mum. What's my problem?

A We suspect you don't have one, apart from anxiety concerning the normal processes of fantasy. (For the record, Freud said that when two people make love there are at least *four* people present, the two in contact and the two they're thinking about). You are also coping in a very practical way with the erotic difficulties presented by your wife's new maternal image. What's so wrong with using a technical means to achieve a sexual purpose? It's not as if your partner is going to breast-feed and dandle babies for the rest of her days.

Q I feel fat because of just having had a baby. I think I'm too fat to make love. Will I ever get thin again?

A Yes, though we can't guarantee your body will regain its old contours. Breast-feeding is a boon because it encourages your uterus at least to return to its former size. Eventually, continued breast-feeding actually draws on the supplies of fat stored up during pregnancy. However, it does take many months to get back into proper shape. Some women look wonderful within six weeks but they are the lucky exceptions. Give yourself at least a year in which to regain a figure and strength. Meanwhile, recognize that no one is actually too fat to make love.

Q After her pregnancy my wife now looks like her mother which appals me. How can I ever feel desire again?

A You are making a very clear statement about your mother-in-law: you cannot stand her. However, you were originally attracted to your wife as a woman who for genetic reasons was likely, when older, to look like her mother. We are left wondering whether the facial similarity is the issue, whether ageing is the issue or whether your relationship with your mother-in-law has become so bad that you now imagine your wife will copy her behaviour? Instead of boycotting your spouse, would it not be more profitable to see a counsellor about *your* mid-life crisis or resolve your dispute with her family?

Q Because I have difficulty conceiving, my gynaecologist has given us 'instructions' on when and how to make love. We are now both beginning to dread 'sex nights'.

A It is an enormous pressure having to make love to order, so if the experience really is threatening your relationship try having a 'fertility holiday' every other month, or for one month every three months. This will give you the breather you need even though conception will inevitably take a bit longer.

Q My husband is so jealous of our baby he makes impossible demands of me. He seems to want sex whenever the baby cries. How shall I deal with him?

A He would appear to feel very insecure in your affections since he became a father. Perhaps this situation contains elements of sinister familiarity for him. It is likely that he has suffered from either parental deprivation himself, or was raised in a welter of jealousy which has become a type of mental second nature. You need to work out a behavioural framework for yourself and stick to it. The first requirement is to show him a lot of attention in ways *other* than sex. Cuddle him, hug him, tell him how pleased you are to see him, tell him you love him. The second requirement is to be firm about his inconsiderate lovemaking demands, just as you would with children who clamoured to get their own way at the wrong time. You might say 'Yes, I'd love to but now is obviously impossible – shall we set the alarm early for the morning?' Your action teaches him on the one hand that he is loved and on the other that your boundaries of decision are secure, and so is he. The third requirement is to help him become more friendly with his child. The more he treats the baby as a person instead of as a symbol of his own deprivation, the sooner he will cease to regard it as a rival. Finally, tell him what time and attention *you* need. If this gets all one-sided it won't be much fun for you.

Q I feel I come a poor second in my husband's affections to our baby daughter. He dotes on her every word and bowel movement.

A Clear statements of your discontent need to be expressed. Arrange time for the two of you to be without baby occasionally and go into your worries about being relegated in his affections. Tell him you feel so needy for love these days precisely because you don't get it any more. Perhaps reinforce your message with mild attempts at humour: 'I know Lucinda is your own true love, my darling, but give your poor wife a break'.

3 The sex life of children

Q **Surely children don't have any feelings of sexuality?**

A Obstetrician William Masters used to devise a game with himself: 'Can I get the cord cut before the kid has an erection?' Close observation confirms that girls, too, show sexual response from birth since the clitoris is the female equivalent of the penis. However, sexual capacity is not the same thing as full sexuality. Young children are endlessly sensual. But their practical sexual responses do not have the same meaning or content as those of adults. When adults want genital stimulation, they express desire, they use fantasy, are aware of their sexual identity, and perhaps the need to bond. When a baby fondles itself, the only motive is the sensuous communication of pure pleasure. So to the mother who is anxious that drying her four-year-old between the legs is a sexual assault, we can only say that the child won't see it that way, though he or she may experience 'general pleasure'.

Of course, later childhood includes a process of specifically *sexual* development, both physical and emotional. On the one hand, a sexually abused child will become too early aware of the adult meanings of sex. He or she may learn to 'ape' the role of seducer. On the other hand, happier children will play sex games together right up to puberty without the fear of exploitation and the loss of self-esteem inherent in incest with an adult. All children project some of their developing desires onto parents in fantasy. Deep down, a son is probably attracted to his Mum, a daughter to her Dad. Successful parents accept this without picking up the invitation so the child gradually realizes his or her sex life has to be enjoyed outside the family.

Q **Can children have orgasms?**

A There is some debate about this. Women watching their children masturbate have perceived times when both boys and girls appear to be satisfied. But small boys cannot ejaculate until they reach puberty and in infancy only have what is described as a 'dry orgasm'. Since for most males orgasm is closely associated with ejaculation (although Eastern sexologists insist the two differ), it is hard to know whether a dry orgasm qualifies. The general agreement is that some (not all) children have pressing needs for genital stimulation but this may not result in complete orgasm until early teens.

Q Should children be taught about orgasm?

A Since innumerable people have become fully functioning human beings without instruction in orgasm (including sexually), there seems no specific reason to focus on it. If a child happens upon climax or something close to it through sex play with other children or through masturbation, this is part of normal spontaneous experience. There is everything wrong, however, with adults taking it upon themselves to 'educate' children by attempting to stimulate them sexually. Sex counsellors (of the bona fide sort) now agree that it is desirable children should know they will receive nice feelings if they touch their genitals. There isn't usually much necessity to tell a boy this since, with no great difficulty, boys find this out for themselves. Girls often don't, however, and present trends are to tell them about their sexual anatomy, and their response, but in very childish terms. The word orgasm doesn't have to be used at this early stage of learning (pre-teens). When you are questioned by the child, a simple 'Yes, doesn't it feel nice?' is probably sufficient.

Q Has any scientific research been carried out into children's sexuality?

A For obvious moral and developmental reasons, no. We've mentioned Dr William Masters' attempt to 'cut the birth cord before the child had an erection'. In fact, he succeeded only half the time. He also noted that all baby girls lubricated vaginally in the first four to six hours of life. Additionally, his later work with adults showed that during sleep, spontaneous erection or vaginal lubrication occurred every 80 to 90 minutes throughout the entire life span.

On the emotional side, there are numerous theories whose usefulness is patent but which cannot be proved. These include the ideas that a child screens from awareness any sexual experience which is too disturbing, yet remains under its influence; that children automatically blame themselves for failures by parents or guardians to maintain the supply of warm, nurturing love; and that a child will grow into an adult whose sexual lifestyle will include a strategy to keep unpleasant memories repressed, choosing friends and lovers on this basis. In other words, adult sexual behaviour nearly always betrays its own origins. For instance, a man who loves to be dominated by sneering women may himself have had a very tough mother whose behaviour at the time he loathed. And yet – although he would like to be fully loved today – he cannot tolerate the uncertainty and unfamiliarity generated by gentle emotions. Part of the reason, we suspect, is that he still lives in hope. If he recreates the childhood scene, and behaves submissively as Mother always wanted, perhaps 'she' will relent and love him for himself rather than his obedience.

Q Why do the genitals of new-borns often appear to have shrunk in size a month or so after birth?

A One theory is that, while still in the womb, babies' genitals are affected by their mothers' adult sex hormones. Once born, this effect is removed and the infant organs cease to be enlarged.

Q If I can't cuddle my new-born baby will this cause harm?

A This depends on how long the lack of cuddling continues. If it's total, yes. Cuddling is an important process in developing your child's mental and emotional response. Research suggests that touch actually creates neural pathways in the brain, allowing your baby to make intelligent connections in its own mind to the outside world. Babies don't communicate in words but through skin messages. Later cuddling may compensate, but do expect problems. Deprived children will always feel affected. They could be suspicious and distrustful. They may be slow to disclose feelings and may have difficulty in later sexual relationships, either because they freeze or because they are overly needy. Experiments with baby monkeys in the 1930s showed that even brain damage could result if the young are brought up deprived of holding, cuddling and hugging.

Q Can a child feel over-hugged?

A There isn't such a thing as sensual overload, if that's what you mean, and it's frankly doubtful whether you can cuddle a baby too much. In the wild, so to speak, you would carry your baby on your back all day. As the child grows up, however, it will indicate when a cuddle feels too smothering.

Q Does 'potty-training' affect a child's later sexual life?

A Some sex researchers believe it does, though it is practically impossible to prove. It would be common sense to suggest you can give your child 'performance anxiety' by trying to teach premature bowel-control and then expressing disappointment when it fails. In later years, such a child may well feel anxious about most undertakings, including sex. 'Will my erection last? Can I delay climax long enough? Shall I be able to let go?', and so on. The parents who can relax about the hits and misses of potty etiquette will probably produce more relaxed kids. So as a general rule, don't start the routine until your child is about 18 months old and then be patient.

Q **When should my child know the facts of life?**

A As soon as he or she is old enough to understand them. Really, the question should be turned round – 'Are there any good reasons for depriving my child of this important information?' Think this through. However, you must always proceed at the child's pace, in the child's own language. So when your 3-year-old asks where babies come from, do not deliver a lecture on sado-masochistic bondage knots. It makes most sense to discuss the facts of life as part of a story when the child is about 2 or 2½, in response to a question or as part of bedtime reading. There are some excellent books to help, full of lines about 'then the little tadpoles swim up inside Mummy' and 'when you were growing in Mummy's tummy', and so forth. If the language seems too complicated, simplify things as you read along. Teaching a child specifically about how his or her genitals work, again following some question or other, is more appropriate at the age of 6 or 7, and girls in particular need this type of education. Bathtime offers a good opportunity for Mother to lend a mirror and explain the function of the different parts. Again, there are lots of books that can fill any gaps in your own knowledge.

Q Can you tell a child too much about sex?

A Of course, by giving too much detail and making a simple story difficult. The worst result of this is not corruption but boredom. Whatever you're talking about, children rapidly tune out if you go beyond them.

Q My children, a boy and a girl, both play with themselves sexually. Does this matter?

A It matters in a positive sense – they are discovering their own anatomy and getting familiar with delightful feelings. This can only be healthy for later love life, but see the next reply.

Q Should I ever stop my child from masturbating?

A Yes — children need to know the boundaries of polite behaviour and this applies to masturbation as it does to anything else. If they start provocative manipulations in front of neighbours, the meter reader or a new babysitter, tell them off in words making it clear that *public display* is the issue. You probably reserve the right to practise masturbation yourself. Your children should not have fewer rights in that respect. But emphasize the need to 'be private', rather than to 'stop that filthy habit'. Also be aware that children may sometimes masturbate in front of others as a rather unhappy 'attention-seeking' behaviour and this could be a sign of disturbance. If so, seek psychological help.

Q Should you ever encourage a child to masturbate?

A No – don't demonstrate, don't assist and don't intervene in their personal development by any sexual act of participation – it amounts to intrusive abuse. Holding a positive attitude towards your child's sexual explorations and answering their questions is enough. Dr Estella Weldon of London's Portman Clinic has described in her books many cases, not just of men taking advantage, but also of women abusing their children – 'the mother who used to masturbate her five children when very young because it was easier than using a dummy to placate them'. If you find you have a problem here, please seek professional help.

Q My child never cuddles me – will this give him problems in later relationships?

A Some children seem less cuddly than others, perhaps because they have no doubts that you do care for them. But just because they don't invite it doesn't mean you should never hug them. Children need to learn the significance of touch as they grow up. One small boy who 'tolerates' his mother's cuddles, but won't offer them himself, nevertheless cradles his cat in his arms, crooning to it lovingly. He knows how to hug and be hugged, and even if he's wary with parents, he should be all right later on when it comes to lovers.

Q My 5-year-old daughter often plays sex games with her friends. Should I interfere?

A The same rule applies as with masturbation – 'Not in front of Granny' who will be distressed, or 'Not in public'. If your daughter is involved by an older girl in this game, she may be carried along at the older child's rate of development rather than her own, which you might discourage. Invite other children as alternative friends if you wish. But otherwise, at this age, the behaviour is pretty typical.

Q Are there any harmful long-term effects of children having sex-play with each other?

A None known, but really it is the context not the action that probably counts most. For instance, a teacher's reaction to some sex prank or other might scar the mind, while the undiscovered prank itself would normally be forgotten. It may be that children who play these games turn out to be sexier than those who don't. But that could be a result of a sensuous nature, rather than what they get up to.

Q My 5-year-old can be very seductive with certain grown-ups. Should I stop her?

A The answer has to be yes, though it is sad that your child cannot find out safely for herself that this behaviour is inappropriate. Friendship with responsible adults would teach her that she is liked for herself, without the need to flirt, but the family climate today shows that too many adults are likely to take advantage.

Q **At what age may a girl become a mother?**

A The plumbing is present at birth, but puberty doesn't usually begin until a girl is 12 or 13. Body weight (between 94 and 103 pounds/43-47kg) is critical. However, puberty and the ability to give birth may not go together. Periods can commence as early as 9 or as late as 17 and yet a girl is probably unlikely to conceive until the menstrual cycles are regular. Studies of primitive societies suggest there may be a natural sterility in very young women for as much as two to three years after the arrival of the first period but newspaper headlines reporting 11-year-old mothers in the West, and those of 9½ in the Arab world, reveal clear and damaging exceptions.

Q **At what age may a boy become a father?**

A On average, male puberty starts at around 12 and continues until a boy is about 17. First ejaculation usually occurs about halfway through the process, at average of 14 or 15, and this is when the young man may biologically become a father, though it's not to be recommended.

Q **When do children stop being sexually innocent?**

A In one sense, they never were (see the first answer in this chapter) but there is a definite increase in sexual consciousness during the puberty process. From about age 10, children start to see more and more sexual meanings in everyday objects such as chimneys and grapefruits.

Q **How soon should I warn my children about potentially dangerous adults?**

A As soon as they are old enough to spend time away from you in a place where they exercise independence. Mostly, this means at a playgroup or school. Good schools already run 'safety awareness' programmes with or without police co-operation. If your school does not, then encourage the teachers to start one.

Q **My husband is embarrassed when he gets an erection in the bathtub with our 2-year-old. What should he do?**

A He should do what feels psychologically comfortable. This may mean putting an end to joint bathing. It may mean making a joke about his penis. It may mean being matter-of-fact about the erection to himself – after all, the child is not going to think father is making an underwater pass. However, if embarrassment persists, he may only feel able to cope by avoiding future joint baths.

Q **When my boys aged 1½ and 2½ undress for the bath my wife often playfully tweaks their penises. Am I right to feel worried about this?**

A No, but your concern does you credit. Mothers around the world are not committing incest when they occasionally do this as part of a washing ritual. For three years of a child's life, nappy-changing parents have to handle their children's genitals and it cannot always be a deadly serious routine (but see page 85).

Q **Our sex life has virtually ceased because our toddler keeps entering our bed. Do we reject her or manage without sex?**

A Your need for sex is one very good reason why a toddler should be encouraged to have a good relationship with its own bed. Once you welcome her in yours, however, the habit can only be broken gradually, yet it's good for her and better for you that this be done. So when she toddles in, get up and lead her gently back to her own bed, saying goodnight again and returning to yours. Don't 'reward the behaviour' by reading to her, supplying drinks and biscuits, or playing games. Just be persistence itself until she falls asleep, and continue the programme till she gives in. Establishing a good *pre-bedtime* routine also helps make the transition from alert activity to drowsiness – so the ideal sequence is romp, bath, story, drink, lights out and sleep. And if all else fails, you can go and make love in the kitchen.

Q Our friends Sara and Keith actually make love while their boy toddler sleeps in their bed. Is this dangerous?

A If he could be crushed, yes! Obviously, as long as he stays asleep he'll know nothing about the actual sex. But there is no guarantee he'll stay sleeping. There have been many children from poor backgrounds who have been forced to share rooms with siblings and parents and who have had to watch their parents making love. Reactions seem immensely varied, from finding it 'beastly' to simply taking it for granted. Perhaps the nature of this reaction really depends on the general quality of the family relationships. There is also the theory that children will be mentally harmed by interpreting sex between their parents as a form of 'fighting'. A few simple words of explanation can put this right, so perhaps the most undesirable aspect of seeing parents make love is that it can interfere with the child's own developing sexual imagination and spoil the spontaneous discovery of sexuality, somehow accelerating or devaluing it. There is an element of exhibitionism in the parents' performance too, involving the child as potential audience. This feels incestuous which is why, in general, we don't usually behave like this.

Q The patter of tiny feet always seems to coincide with our climax. How do we explain what we are doing? Should we even try to explain?

A It depends on how old your child is and what he or she has actually witnessed. To the very young, explaining that Daddy and Mummy are playing together and having fun should be adequate. If the child is getting on for 3 or so, it would be perfectly reasonable, and truthful, to say 'Daddy and Mummy are making love', especially if there has been a lot of movement under the covers. If Junior comments on any distressing cries you may have uttered, give reassurances that you were making noises of happiness, not of fright. Then say it's time to go back to bed.

Q My 9-year-old recently wandered into the bedroom and saw us making love. He's not a baby any more and understood what we were doing. But he hasn't said a word about it and I haven't known if I should say anything to him. Should I keep quiet?

A It's a pity you weren't able to talk about this event at the time. Now such a discussion will feel strained and may resolve nothing. Your best bet is probably not to discuss the incident itself but the fact that you need some new family rules about knocking on bedroom doors and waiting for a firm 'Come in' or 'Come back later' response. This would give you the chance to add: 'By starting this new rule, Johnny, we could avoid you getting embarrassed about barging in on our lovemaking', and by making this statement you help Johnny in several ways. He hears that you think the issue is mainly a practical problem. He is given permission to talk about it in everyday terms. And he hears you acknowledge that possibly the event raised some difficult feelings for him which you respect and wish to allay. (Make sure you also agree to knock on *his* door before barging in there too.)

Q I want to put a lock on our bedroom door so that we regain our privacy. How will my 9-year-old react?

A She is likely to pick up whatever feelings you send out. So if you're consumed with guilt about it, she'll feel aggrieved. If you can persuade yourself that privacy is important, and your action justifiable, then your child will regard the change as just a domestic nuisance she can learn to accept.

Q Our 15-year-old's bedroom is next door to ours. I have recently become anxious that he will recognize the sounds of our lovemaking and this is putting me off sex in a big way. Now my husband is complaining about my lack of interest. What can I do?

A First, try to understand that a son is perfectly able to cope with the idea that his mother makes love even though he may never talk about it. There is nothing abnormal about a child knowing his parents still like sex and it is considerably healthier than thinking they never go near each other. Second, if necessary and practicable, shuffle the bedrooms around. Third, get a noise-free bed, insulate the walls and practise silent climaxes (which can be fun). The REAL alternative, however, is to ask yourself why the problem has arrived now, after some 15 years. Are you having trouble accepting your child's maturity? Are you angry with your husband for some other reasons? Have you lost confidence elsewhere? You need to put an 'emotional detective' into your head.

Q **How will my young kids feel if they know my new man stays the night?**

A Curious, cross maybe, but unlikely to be shocked. Children who feel comfortable at home will understand that someone else would enjoy spending time in it. If they see your man cuddle you in the kitchen or living room, they won't necessarily think it odd that the same thing happens in the bedroom. Very young children won't infer a sexual meaning to the behaviour in any case. Older ones who do know what a new head on your pillow implies may be angry if their lives have been recently disturbed but will be much less affected by overnight stays than by talk of step-fathers. If you feel your kids should not know about a lover unless he's ready to marry you, then we are really talking about your needs, not the children's. You are setting this as a boundary around your emotions. Perhaps the very desire to let him stay all night means your feelings are becoming much more serious?

Q **My ex-husband has three different girlfriends and I am worried about letting my children stay and see him in bed with them.**

A Assuming he holds no orgies, the children will still feel all right so long as *their* status in Daddy's house remains secure. His women friends won't make much difference apart from providing someone to talk to. The only circumstance to bother you would be if the children in any way became sexually involved with the girlfriends. This is pretty unlikely but should it be the case, you would be absolutely right in keeping them firmly with you. We guess you really feel bothered about him dating any girl, let alone three.

Q **Does my divorce mean my children will follow my example?**

A It's an even money bet. Your behaviour may give them the courage to cancel a lousy relationship (when they grow up) *or* incline them to seek a lifetime bond by contrast with the experience provided by your example. Either way, you should not use their hypothetical marital future as a reason for punishing yourself today. Divorce is tough enough already.

Q **My 8-year-old son has to share a bed with me at present until I can afford larger accommodation. Is this harmful?**

A It is not ideal but if space is such a problem that two separate beds cannot be used, then for the time being it's unavoidable. Children, like adults, need their own private territory. As he gets older, your son may tend to focus his sexual fantasies on you more strongly than is helpful (watching you undress, etc). For now, the situation is just tenable – but it won't be in two or three years' time.

Q **My 10-year-old daughter wants to share a bed with her best friend from school – should I allow this?**

A If the room contains only a double bed, then it's possible the girls literally want to be close. If the room has two single beds and they only want to use one of them, they are asking to be sensually close too, albeit innocently. How *you* feel about that will decide the issue.

Q My husband has stopped the friendly wrestling matches he used to enjoy with our son, now aged 11, because they gave him an erection. Is he right to stop?

A Yes. There comes a time when age and sex affect family horseplay for adult as well as child. Usually, the child knows it is time to stop before the parent does.

Q I'm the father of a 10-year-old girl who still kisses me full on the lips. Should she be doing this now she's growing up so rapidly and already has breasts?

A She seems comfortable, you seem embarrassed. The reason for stopping, therefore, would be for your sake, so don't believe it's for her protection. If you could admit this, maybe the pressure would ease. She'll give it up *in any case* when she's ready.

Q Should I stop cuddling my 10-year-old son? I'm his mother.

A Not unless he objects. Some children happily go on cuddling forever. Some come back to it in their 20s. Some never really learned to start.

Q When does family kissing and cuddling become incest?

A When the child's body is touched for sexual gratification (especially face, breasts, genitals and anus).

Q My 8-year-old son and 9-year-old daughter appear to be playing sexual games together – something they used to do when they were 4 and 5. Should they be separated?

A Hard to be sure. The children may be fine, but one could be bullying the other. Since this can be very destructive, it is probably better to separate them tactfully if the games go on.

Q My 9-year-old son has been looking at pornographic magazines which some other child brought into school. What should I do?

A In each school year, one child will prove precocious by showing off to his friends sexually. Possessing and circulating porn is a typical instance. But what you ought to do depends on who you are.

Remember that the ages from 8 to 10 seem to show a special growth in sexual awareness. Long before the mass distribution of glossy booklets, small children arrived in school with suggestively-shaped carrots, potatoes, parsnips and tomatoes (or 'love-apples') to provide the opportunity for a general snigger. If you know your child is discussing explicit sex, it would certainly be a good time to make it clear that furtive sniggers are not the same thing as the mood necessary for lovemaking – that sex can be many things but it tends to be best when carried out in a gratifying relationship. Some parents believe it is important to be accepting of such literature for fear of conferring 'forbidden status' on the material, rendering it more not less desirable. Others tolerate sex porn but reject depictions of violence. In Japan, pornography featuring hara-kiri and decapitation is often acceptable while photos of genitals are not. In still other parts of the world, parents forbid all such items. In effect, community standards vary with the community.

Perhaps the most important rule for the health of your child is that these standards should not be hypocritical. If you order him or her never to look at the stuff while at the same time hoarding a pile of magazines under your bed (which anyone can discover) then you are simply driving your family into confusion. One girl found her Catholic father's hoard of sex videos in the attic believing them to be tapes of her 18th birthday party. She left home forever immediately after playing them.

Q My 6-year-old daughter is always encouraging the other kids in school to look up her skirt. What's this about?

A It may mean she is precociously sexual, a difficult concept in this age of abuse-awareness, yet some children have simply learned to exhibit themselves for fun. It may mean she badly needs approval because she isn't getting enough at home. It may be her way of trying to buy influence with a group of friends who are pushing each other further and further in a series of 'dares'. It would be wise to consider the innocent explanations first since these are most common. You should also talk things through with the relevant teacher or playground attendant since they may have helpful information to offer. Whatever the cause, it would be useful to ask your child to behave with more discretion.

Q Our 11-year-old daughter started her periods when she was 10, has a womanly figure and talks of nothing but boys. How can we stop her growing up too fast?

A You can't. Her physical development has happened and her interest in boys is undoubtedly reinforced by this early sexual maturity. Your best course is to try to build acceptance of these facts into your relationship with her. Rather than force her to hang around street corners with boys she is attracted to, make it clear they are welcome in your home. It may be possible to do some useful trade-offs. Suggest she spends one evening with a boy in return for one evening with the homework. Telling her she is too young to date, or forcing her to wear skirts down to her ankles, will only breed rebellion – and possibly pregnancy.

Q Will my 12-year-old daughter be influenced by her sexually experienced boyfriend?

A To an extent, but it mainly depends on her own character and maturity. Some young women who are very much *pre-sexual* will feel repulsed by unwanted erotic advances. Others will behave according to their upbringing. If you have dominated her life with smothering restrictions, she is likely to do whatever *he* wants, and whatever peer-group pressure encourages. If you have allowed her to develop self-confidence, then she has a real freedom of decision ahead. Many mothers find it more difficult to talk to their daughters round about puberty but it is a key time to exchange views – including your view that perhaps serious dating might wait a while. Even if you disagree with her, and she with you, she needs to believe you care supportively about her feelings.

Q Children at my daughter's school date at 10, 11 and 12. I strongly disapprove of this because I know it gets in the way of study and my daughter isn't interested in boys anyway. How can I stop her following the herd?

A Fitting in with friends at school is a central part of growing up. Being prevented can make you lonely and isolated. If your daughter is really so different from her schoolmates and would be happier leading the life of a more traditional schoolgirl, then she is at the wrong school. Explore the possibilities of transferring her to somewhere more suitable. She may prefer an all-girls school, if this can be found, especially if she has academic inclinations since research shows girls do better intellectually when separated from boys! If such a change is impossible, then your best course is to make home activities so attractive that she will prefer to spend more time with the family, possibly even importing some of her schoolfriends.

Q When should you stop bathing a child? My son is 10 but left to himself emerges from the bath as dirty as when he went in.

A Go into a transition stage now. Let him do the bathing, but you do the checking. If you can manage to instil a self-cleansing routine whatever the degree of protest, then while developing his independence you are also working for hygiene. In other words, show him that not washing properly gives *him* hassles, and send him back if the standard isn't met. Subtly point out that the checking can be abolished along with the dirt.

Q **I am aware there comes a time when children need to know more than the basic facts of life. At what age should I tell them about VD, homosexuality, cunnilingus etc?**

A With so much public anxiety about AIDS, for example, we're surprised that you haven't had some family discussion of the problems of sexually transmitted diseases, if only in simple form. It's a good idea to use press stories to introduce these topics from time to time.

Homosexuality is always in the news. Lovemaking techniques, such as oral sex, are obviously not quite in the same category. The golden rule is to let your children ask the questions when and if they need to, then give plain and truthful replies. For the rest, you would do well to make certain books available in the home – books on teenage worries, growing up, contraception and sex education. Leave these around the house but also be seen reading them yourself – so the kids get a chance to raise issues naturally.

4   A divorce in your sex life

Q It's been nine months since my wife left but I still feel dead inside.

A Some in your situation grieve for months, some for two to three years. It is complicated by several other psychological processes, including that of 'denial'. For example, a man may be unable to admit to real distress so he buries himself in work. On the surface, he is untroubled but if you consider how *compelled* he feels to stay busy, you will realise he is prolonging the period of 'grief-related stress' almost indefinitely. Some people feel short-lived grief whose brevity is genuine – they didn't care too much for the person who is gone. But yours is different – you hurt and the feelings may include memories of previous leavings; plus a current sense of rejection; a sense of failure; a sense of confusion; a sense of inadequacy; of loneliness; of emasculation; of impotence; of humiliation; and a profound sense of injustice. If any of this fits your bill, a great deal of depressive activity is going to occur so do try to accept the apparent lack of progress. Events in life always happen faster than our feelings can register them. You can only adapt to this change by counting your sorrows and losses one by one over many days with a lot of protest. Just keep on telling yourself that if you can let the tears and curses flow, the underlying feelings will gradually be eased into exhaustion.

Q Since my husband left to become a born-again bachelor I have dated 17 men and been to bed with nine of them. My friends are horrified I am dating so soon and so often and I'm surprised at myself. Why am I being so promiscuous?

A You probably *don't* have a death-wish, but with the rate of HIV infection rising amongst heterosexuals, it's something to consider. More likely you feel you cannot bear the emotional implications of being deserted. No one, of course, finds this easy. But in your grief and panic you are repeatedly soliciting a mixture of messages from men. On the one hand, you are simply asking for reassurance that they want you. On the other, perhaps feeling of little value in yourself, you are inviting them to confirm that anyone can have you. Possibly, you are defying convention too. Since your husband broke the marriage vows, why should you worry about who has whom? More positively, maybe you're also feeling a huge sense of liberation, or want to make up for lost time?

However, remember that children who cannot talk about their distress because they have been abused often become promiscuous. They pay the sexual price in order to obtain love. It's 'how they've been trained'. We wonder whether you also feel an overwhelming ache for support from others which you cannot put into words and that's why you settle for serial sexual embraces? Maybe you've also been conditioned from childhood to hide your inner distress? Either way, don't condemn yourself for trying a solution that may not be working. We all want to turn our backs on pain. But there probably is an alternative involving treating yourself like a human being who can admit she's angry and sad rather than acting out the tough cookie who takes on all-comers.

Q After my husband walked out, his business
partner turned up to console me, then made a
pass. How crass can men be?

A We'd better not answer that, though it might have
been different had his partner been married to the
woman in the previous question. Suffice it to say
that many men find the idea of a married woman
in distress very affecting. Part of consolation
consists of touch, the comforting hand, the warm
hug, the rubbing of the shoulders, the holding of
the waist. Some men mistakenly believe this kind
of intimacy should always lead to sexual
intimacy. Perhaps they cannot refrain from feeling
aroused? Some men do know better, but try it on
anyway because they are heels. And some men
are ineradicable sexists who assume any woman
is sexually available when a 'possessing' male is
absent. Obviously, the pass only added to *your*
distress.

Q Can you be sexual while still grieving? My heart is breaking for the marriage that has ended but I miss sex so much. I'm so restless. I fear I'll be driven to look for a man.

A Human reactions are uniquely varied. Where grief for one is depressing and sexless, for another it is utterly arousing, perhaps through anger or heightened excitement of the sort that makes your adrenalin pump. As you are used to relying on your husband for comfort, you may also be naturally drawn to others for the same reason, and the same depth of comfort. Old reflexes die hard. If you don't already masturbate, why not learn to do so? It would enable you to 'grieve in dignity' without having to go on the hunt at what you may feel is an inappropriate time.

Q My wife has ended our marriage and all my mates at work keep joking about me having all the sexual opportunities in the world, but I've never felt less like it.

A They are talking wishfully about themselves, so tune it out – you can be sure they wouldn't be so chipper if they really felt as you do. You need to work on the idea that just because your wife no longer wants to be married to you it doesn't follow that you are intolerable. In other words, she holds only one opinion on the situation. Sex and depression are incompatible so don't be surprised to feel 'dormant' until the clouds begin to clear. This will almost certainly include the time up to a formal settlement of a divorce or separation.

Q I've got lots of boyfriends to go out with but I can't have an orgasm with anyone anymore. One day I'd like to remarry but I see this as an obstacle.

A Perhaps that's one of its purposes? You see, if you never remarry you never run the risk of history repeating itself. If your orgasmic response fails to return, you won't ever have to let a man get close enough to reject you again, will you? Certainly, if you were always orgasmic up until the divorce it is something about the break-up itself which now prevents you from letting your body go. Possibly the second Mr Right hasn't come along. But maybe he *can't* until you learn to voice the mistrust and misery generated by the first. See whether one of your more sympathetic boyfriends could not play listener as well as lover while you tell him the story of your break-up. In order to let go physically and one day remarry you are going to have to allow these feelings to see the light of day.

Q Since my divorce I've got in with a crowd of very extrovert people who go in for naturism, swapping and discreet orgies. As a result, I've really discovered myself sexually although I still feel very lonely.

A So we hear you saying this new social set hasn't been able to satisfy *all* your intimacy needs. Has it therefore served its purpose, which was to put you in touch with that exhibitionistic side of your nature repressed by matrimony? If so, listen to the message. Are you ready to move on – which would decrease some of the health risks you've been running too?

Q Having been solitary after my divorce, I am shocked to find I've fallen in love with another *woman*. I want our kisses and caresses to go on forever but I'm also alarmed in case they do and I become a lifelong lesbian. I'd like to end up remarried. Will I?

A Probably, since you have always seen your life in a heterosexual framework and your relationship with this woman is based on a deep need for a sustaining womanly relationship at a time of trouble. Whether or not such friendships become sexual depends almost as much on chance and your level of inhibition as anything else. The English novelist Joanna Trollope writes of similar motives among the still-attached:

Married women in their 20s with small demanding children, and a husband building his career, do not have time to think. Then, as they approach 30 and realize they have never got their teeth into their own life, a tremendous loneliness can descend. Women who are neither homosexual nor unfaithful by nature are ripe plums for the picking.

Doesn't this sound a little like you? We hope you will always be friends with your current lover whose gift of herself is like a therapy yet if you also want a man in your life the only obstacles are practical – like finding him, then juggling your diary.

Q I've met a man who in many ways would be a perfect new husband except he never seems to want sex. He's making me feel like a dirty old woman.

A Either he is too low-sexed for you to have a decent relationship with him or he has particular sensitivities and hesitations concerning your past (or his present) marital condition. You have to decide whether it's still promising enough when he divulges his reasons for leaving you cold.

Q My new partner is a great 'catch', having a reputation as a ladies' man and excellent good looks. However, I am surprised by the infrequency of his sexual demands although he assures me it will be better when he is no longer so entangled in the lives of others.

A In which case, we suggest you suspend judgement until he is holding *you alone*. You need to know for sure whether he can discover enough ego-gratification in a one-to-one relationship to make it sexually satisfying. So don't just buy the advertising, or forget the risks.

Q Tongues wag very easily in our small town. There's gossip about me circulating already although I've only been out with two men since my divorce. I want a normal love life but I can't stand the sexual innuendo.

A Yet after tongues have wagged, what can they do but repeat themselves? When they've said their piece, most gossips come to accept that life goes on, regularly or otherwise. So our question is about your feelings. Are you really comfortable with renewed dating, or are you projecting your very own reactions onto the rest of the neighbourhood? Run a test. Take a date in the *next* town, or even the city. See whether you still feel uncomfortable in an environment where no one *can* be talking about you.

111

Q I don't know what to think. My manfriend courts me in the most extravagant way, wining and dining me, being elaborately romantic, bringing presents of bon-bons, telling me I'm unique, and so on. He holds my hand, kisses and cuddles whenever possible, wants to neck like a teenager, gets me terrifically turned on but only once in every two or three months takes anything further. Then we go back to my place, make love and it's awful. He's a damp squib compared to his build-up. We're all done inside ten minutes. I won't see him for a week, then the whole rigmarole starts over again.

A His sexual abilities seem grossly inferior to his courtship techniques but you don't know the reason for this because you have never asked him. He could be hooked on romance, finding the 'chase' more interesting than the 'kill'. He may sincerely *want* his lovemaking to live up to the preamble but is hampered by premature ejaculation which he doesn't know how to deal with. It is not inconceivable he actually thinks the sex is splendid. It may be for him since, however damp your squib, he is obviously getting an orgasm out of it. Does he *know* that you aren't? All the way through your description, we hear of him making the moves but if you're dissatisfied it is up to you to take responsibility for the problem. Ask him if he would *like* you to have an orgasm? Then show him how.

Q Now divorced, I am quite self-sufficient. I cook and clean with the best of them and my kids are well-adjusted. I need women as friends and lovers but don't need a replacement wife. When women find out I'm not prepared to offer marriage, they get angry and accuse me of 'only being after one thing'.

A Life is most difficult when twin paranoias meet. You are as guilty of stereotyping women as they seem to be in libelling you. Can we start again? So far, you have mostly met females with matrimony on their minds. Perhaps you've been unlucky or perhaps you are over-selecting from this group by dating women younger than yourself? Try an older (and wiser?) age group – women who are not necessarily looking for shared homes and children because 'they have already done all that'. Given current divorce trends, supply is not the problem you suppose. And try not to feel persecuted if marriage still arises as an issue. It's a popular custom.

Q I'm very aware of the need for safe sex if I'm going to have several partners now that I'm divorced but the awful business of using condoms (sheaths, as we used to call them) is ruining everything. First, I'm often embarrassed to produce them. Second, they spoil my pleasure. It really is like making love in a rubber mac. I don't get enough stimulation on my penis to make me come. So what do I do – die sexually fulfilled or live frustrated? Is there anything in between?

A Yes, there's the idea that 'screwing' isn't the only sexual option. There is also lovemaking using the hands. 'Manual magic' can provide many women with greater satisfaction than conventional intercourse. And if you haven't tried the combination of condom, KY Jelly, your lover's oscillating fingers encompassing your penis while her other hand toys with your testicles you've never known what it is to beg for mercy. Once you are used to coming in this fashion, you'll be more likely to associate rubber prophylactics with ecstasy. We also wonder whether a little of your 'orgasmic reticence' is common-or-garden anxiety about women in this post-divorce period. Are you sure you're actually ready to be sexual?

Q My manfriend screams (literally) when I touch him anywhere below the belt. I'm used to turning a man on by caressing his penis (especially with my ex), and I find this boyfriend's sensitivity *so* limiting. Could he change?

A Yes – provided he's 'handled' in the right way. A light touch appears to produce a reaction of extreme nervousness, no doubt fostered by childhood memories of ticklishness or embarrassment. A firm touch without sudden moves, carried out slowly, would have a very different effect. He will need time to adjust to you in the same way that you will have to adapt to your new erotic circumstances. Look him in the eyes and tell him gently that your hand is now, very safely, and lovingly, going to move lower . . .

Q My womanfriend is only a few years younger than me but she is a club athlete who runs 12 miles a day. During intercourse she wants me to ram into her harder and faster than I am able. It either makes me come, or makes me gasp. Either way, she's left complaining.

A Well, you can't do what she demands, can you? Tell her the score. Then announce your resolve to take up jogging but in the meantime could she possibly tolerate a lot more oral sex, hand-held vibrator pleasure or mutual masturbation than she is accustomed to? No? Well at the very least get her to climb on top and do all the hard work of pelvic grinding while you concentrate on pacing a climax.

Q My new guy is much younger than my husband, much more athletic and very vigorous. He goes on with sex so long I get cramp. Do you know ways in which I can speed up his climax?

A We take your point, although cramp could be prevented by choosing more comfortable coupling positions such as rear entry or with you semi-seated on the side of the bed. Courtesans down the ages, occasionally remembering that time is money, have perfected little tricks to make a man lose his cool. They include: stroking or gently squeezing his testicles; tickling his perineum (the sensitive zone between testicles and anus); inserting a finger, toe or other (safe) object into his rectal opening; digital massage of the prostate gland (just insert a finger and ask him where to probe and press); pinching of the nipples; light smacking of the buttocks; mild verbal abuse and use of four-letter language; recitation of the fantasies you know he finds overwhelming (such as three-in-a-bed with the woman he next most fancies after you); putting your panties over his head, and making him taste your love-juice, saying it is 'all for him'. Please don't do *all* this to one man! Use your wits to discover which actions are, and which are not, to his personal taste.

Q I left my husband when I finally found I preferred women to men. For three years I've been in a stable partnership with Elizabeth and my two toddlers. Things are fine now but will my children be affected by our unconventional household when they grow up?

A Yes, but primarily by its 'quality' of relationship, not its 'type'. Questions like 'Why do we have two mummies instead of a mummy and a daddy?' can be answered literally and honestly. You make it clear to the children that while in general men and women fall in love, sometimes this happens between two people of the same sex. You also stress very strongly that every child does indeed have a daddy and try if possible to maintain good contacts with him (though this may sometimes prove difficult). The children will understand early on that biologically you always need a daddy to make a baby but socially it happens that some daddies live away from their children, or start new families with new mummies. The principal social study of the children in lesbian relationships, by the way, concluded that upbringing had made no major difference to their understanding of the social world, or expectations of life, compared to their peers in heterosexual families.

Q After my divorce I fell in love with two men, Michael and Andrew. I didn't plan it this way. I have sex with them both, at different times, and it all feels perfectly natural. They differ from each other (one is practical, the other artistic) and together they make my life complete. It all feels deliciously real. Is it?

A Well, something is bugging you but we mainly suspect it's the effect of seizing your freedom for the first time in your life. If our assumption is correct, you are the sort of person who got married straight from the parental home. In important respects, you did not have a teenage. There was no time to 'stand and stare', break the rules, sow wild oats, kick over the traces, sulk in your bedroom, play one boyfriend off against another and experiment with the powers of sex. Lots of individuals, particularly women, actually have their teenage phase 'out of synch', post-divorce when their children are nearly grown up and they themselves are thinking about guess what? – going back to college. We suggest it's never too late to be an adolescent. We knew one man who actually retired at 64 but went back to work in order to 'be a bit of a lad again'.

Q A couple of false starts after my divorce and now I've settled down nicely with an older man. Unfortunately, something always seems to be missing, sexually speaking. It is so different from my married love life.

A Yes, and it will be. You have to realize that with each new partner we effectively start again from scratch, or may have to. It's always possible to ask for what you want in bed so long as you obey the golden rule. State your preference, not your intolerance. Say, 'That's quite nice but I really want you to lick me in the ear'. Say, 'What I really want next is for you to go down on me, is that on the menu?' Say, 'I feel desperate for you to put your right index finger in your mouth then on the very tip of my clitoris while you move your penis in and out of me ever so slowly – can I have what I want?' These statements will boost your lover's ego, as well as giving him traffic directions. Never say he's inept, because you will only ensure he becomes so. If it doesn't work, of course, you will have to reconsider his eligibility.

Q Sex with my girlfriend was great till we decided to marry. Now I'm always thinking about my ex-wife and it puts me off my stroke.

A The prospect of a second marriage is re-awakening the anxieties connected with your first. Sex is an expression of great intimacy and it is in your most intimate self that you feel vulnerable, hence the withdrawal. Voice your fears in simple sentences starting 'I feel anxious about getting married again because my first wife used to . . . she made me feel . . . she said to me that I . . . I began to worry that . . .' If you fill in the blanks your partner will be able to show you what a different woman she is.

Q **Are there any men who want a *relationship* rather than sex? I'm so tired of dinner being served up as foreplay.**

A Yes, but there aren't very many of them. Why not try to build a circle of friends who go out in a group, play games, take holidays and share more than basic ideas?

Q **I'm going out with an old friend who had marriage problems. When he first undressed in front of me, I got an inkling of the trouble – his penis is tiny. We didn't have intercourse this time, nor did he noticeably get an erection. Do you suppose he can?**

A The strangest things can happen with some of the least likely lovers. A short penis is no deterrent to wonderful lovemaking (homosexual women can rub mere *pubes* together and climax repeatedly). If anything, sheer length is less important than girth but a man with clever brains and sensitive fingers can drive almost any woman wild. Moreover, small cocks tend to erect more than large ones and many men over 30 cannot get much of an erection until their genitals are touched by hand anyway, so please suspend your snap judgement.

Q After a miserable year alone, I have finally found a wonderful lady to love. The only trouble is that for the first time in my life my damned equipment refuses to function. Try as I will, I cannot keep my erection and I've repeatedly let her down.

A Oh no you haven't, your body is behaving perfectly normally in refusing to function when you yourself feel so anxious, nervous and scared. You would actually be letting this woman down if you were able to behave like a 'robot-gigolo'. We classify your problem as 'divorce impotence' because it's so uniformly widespread. What's happening is that you are trying to be sexual before you feel comfortable. You need to become much more accustomed to the relationship before you can perform freely. You need to be helped to heal the wounds to your pride and confidence caused by the loss of your marriage. This means 'on with the massage and all-night cuddles – off with the bungled attempts at over-hasty intercourse'.

We're sure your equipment is fine. It's been working reliably for years. Just pace your expectations. After all, an erection is only produced by pumping more blood into the hollow spaces of the penis than, for the time being, is allowed to leave. The process is *hydraulic* not muscular. A neural reflex is the means of controlling it, not an act of will. When conscious, you can always raise your arm. All you can do to get an erection is create the circumstances in which one is likely, then await developments. And if you are anxious, nervous and scared, your erection-centre *cannot* issue the necessary commands to move the blood around your body. After all, it's still needed in the big muscles of the arms and legs to help you fight or run away if the danger is overwhelming in a primitive biological sense.

Q As a divorcee, I've teamed up with several men who have just come out of a marriage themselves. Every single one of them has been impotent when we went to bed. Is it divorced men, or is it me?

A It could be both. It could be neither. If the men have had 'castrating' relationships with previous wives, that might be your answer. Equally, the problem may be due to long-term sexual dysfunction on their part; organic disease; drug or alcohol dependency or any one of a hundred personal male anxieties (see the answer to the previous question). We doubt if you lack attractiveness otherwise you would hardly have been dated in the first place, but if the 'cause' lies on your side you might think about your own ability to welcome penetration. Do you tend to tense up, making entry problematic? (If you do, this can make an erection disappear very rapidly indeed.) Are you still emotionally bruised by your marriage or some other lover so that although your head says let's make love, your heart says let's sabotage its performance? Next time you meet a lovely man with a flaccid appendage (if you do), hie him off to a sex therapist and see how quickly the techniques of 'sensate focus' reveal who does and who doesn't want what.

Q My ex-husband used to complain that my genitals smelled bad even though I washed meticulously. I feel so nervous about this now that I daren't get close to men. Could I have a sexual disease?

A Possible, but not so likely. Your doctor or clinic could decide. For example, if you had recurrent thrush (candida albicans) we're sure you'd realize. It's more plausible to think that your husband was either out of sympathy with your natural sex musk, or somewhat averse to women. If the latter, he was probably given this hang-up by parents with a purity-fetish. Contrary to your fear, the majority of men *are* turned on by a woman's *cassolette* (literally, her 'perfume-box').

Q The trouble with being divorced, in your 40s and female, is that there are very few single men around. I find myself at 42 going with a youth of 22. I'm staggered he should want me but he does. In fact, he can't get enough of me and it's lovely. Am I daft in hoping we could marry? My friends sniff about me playing with a toy boy.

A Yes, but a toy boy is a male 'bimbo'. He's good for a few one-night stands but you cannot generate a relationship. Clearly, you do relate to your young man and he to you. That said, have no illusions. It might end tomorrow. But there are many good reasons why a young man stays content with an older woman for many years – because she has so much to teach him; because she is non-threatening; because she understands and tolerates his more difficult behaviour. Just take it 'day by day' and remind yourself that friends may suffer from latent envy.

Q My boyfriend is separated with custody of his two small sons. He is very worried about the boys' view of him as a sexual person, and for this reason I find myself being driven home at 2 a.m. after we've made love when I really need to go to sleep, or I'm made to stand outside the front door at 6 a.m. so the kids will imagine I've dropped in for breakfast (complete with nightie and toothbrush!) Should I give him up?

A If you want to marry him and think he might agree, it would seem worth soldiering on. If not, why be used?

Q I went home with this older woman the other night and found myself next morning clutching the sheets around my neck as her 8 and 10-year-old children came in and formally shook hands with me. I found this hard to take and I got worried. Surely it can't be good for kids to find a strange man in their mother's bed? P.S. – she has a mirror on her bedroom ceiling.

A It's impossible to say. Some children have such secure relationships with those who care for them that they understand and accept sexuality for what it is – a universal human condition. Others in this situation may become disturbingly enraged. All we do know for sure is that when confronted by your new mistress's family you began to perspire. Perhaps a partner with two 'knowing' children and a desire to watch herself making love in a ceiling mirror is more than you are ready to take on?

Q How does anyone with children manage to have a sex life after divorce? I have to baby-sit mine most evenings. If I am lucky enough to have visitors, the kids are always sitting round saying 'And when are *you* leaving?'

A Invest more effort in finding reliable baby-sitters and inform grandparents they will more frequently be having small relatives to stay in the months ahead. Put your friends with children on a baby-sitting swap-rota – so you all get nights off in turn. If you haven't got such friends, make them through contacts at your children's schools.

Q Knowing my kids are in the next room, even though they are asleep, really puts me off lovemaking with my new man.

A If possible, swap the rooms around in your house so the kids are not next door to you. Otherwise, invest in sound proofing, door locks and more baby-sitters (check their references). You owe yourself (and your kids) a normal life.

Q My new fiance kisses and cuddles me a lot. Although I wouldn't let anything sexual happen in front of the children, I do want them to see that someone loves and values me because their father didn't. My parents tell me I'm upsetting the children, though.

A If we are just talking cuddles and caresses, fine. Your view is spot on. If you are talking about long necking sessions on the sofa with you hardly ever coming up for air and a lot of wriggling, then perhaps they can't deal with that. Why not ask the kids what they feel?

Q My manfriend seems as interested in my older daughter as he is in me. I keep telling myself not to be jealous or to start imagining trouble, but I do worry. She's 14 and *so* well-developed.

A You could tell your boyfriend that whether or not anything is 'going on' between them, you are very uncomfortable with the way he pays her attention. You could explain that you would like him to alter this behaviour. You could also say that if he finds himself unable to alter his behaviour, there is little future in the relationship, so much are your feelings becoming distressed.

Q My second husband is so different from my first that they are virtual opposites. This is confusing my children when it comes to family rules on sex, morality, swearing, politeness, dirty jokes and so on. Their father is a prude. My new man is very liberal. How will they know what is right?

A Given the freedom to develop, your children will take what they want and need from *all* their parents. What is most important is that someone (you?) respects their attempts to make sense of the doctrinal conflicts. Their father probably cannot be influenced. Your present husband should be. Ensure he lives by his own lights but does not constantly shoot down alternative views. Intellectual challenge is useful but if he really wants the kids to follow his lead, point out how his example must *feel* tolerant, not just sound it. If your children end up realizing that 'different families have different rules', with some allowance for social overlap, you won't have done a bad job.

5   Teenage sex life

Part one: Teenagers' questions

Q **I foolishly rang one of those numbers you see advertised in London phone booths and had a topless massage plus 'hand relief' from a prostitute. I have never had a girlfriend. I am now desperately worried I could have caught AIDS, though my brain tells me this is unlikely. I cannot get this fear out of my head.**

A Yes, it's most unlikely you will acquire HIV from a sex 'massage'. What you have picked up instead is an enormous dose of guilt. You feel your behaviour was wrong. Inside, you believe you ought to be punished. Yet it would be more helpful to try and understand yourself. There are some obvious thoughts to consider. Did it happen because you are shy about making contact with women? Does this mean you need to improve your social skills? Do you underestimate your ordinary need for physical closeness anyway? If beneficial, consider the attitudes of your own family towards sex. Did they encourage or inhibit you? Best of all, try to forgive yourself for the sin of curiosity – now you know how a hooker makes money out of men.

Q **My youngest sister is getting keen on a boy whom I know to be really awful – you know, the sort who boasts about his sexual conquests. What can I do?**

A You have a choice. If you warn your sister off, she will probably resent you for months as well as flinging herself into the arms of an unworthy lover. If you bite your tongue, she *may* still make a painful mistake but it will be entirely hers and one from which she can learn. Whatever the outcome, the helpful course is for you to be supportive. If she does have a hard time, you can do your best to introduce her to other young men who are not compiling their erotic memoirs.

Q **There's this boy I know who lives three doors away. How can I make him like me? I really like him.**

A You can't make anyone like you. It's up to them whether they do that or not. What you can do is try to make friends with this young man. You need to tell yourself in advance it's possible he already possesses a girlfriend, or that for five years he's only kissed his computer. In other words, don't make assumptions about success. Start a conversation one day to see whether you two do have things in common, remembering to smile, make eye contact, listen with your whole face and ask general, 'open' questions like 'Hello, how are you doing? . . . How's it going? . . . And what's happening with you, then?'

Q One day I really fancy this boy, the next I can't bear the idea of him touching me. I desperately want a boyfriend, but how will I keep one if I feel like this? My friends don't have this trouble.

A One of the perils of puberty is bad timing. This works in several ways. For instance, of three girls aged 13 one may be slim-hipped, short and flat-chested; the second may be approaching adult height, showing breast-buds and her first pubic hairs; the third may be a tall, rounded, fully-developed, confident female. How can they all be expected to lead similar lives?

The second area of bad timing concerns these 'in-between' feelings. You are no longer a child, so some days you want an adult lifestyle. But you are not yet fully grown-up, so on other days you only want to be looked after. On Monday, you are desperate for a proper love affair. On Tuesday, you want to sit at home, eat cereal and watch children's TV. Emotionally, you are not quite ready for regular dating. Don't worry. This stage doesn't last forever. Before long, you'll meet someone with whom a friendship will just take off. Often when you feel out of your depth with people it is because they are trying to take things too fast for you anyway. So respect your instincts. Only allow serious petting when two conditions are right – when you yearn for it but also feel comfortable with its intensity.

Q A girl on the bus the other day looked at me as if she fancied me, and I looked back. Does this mean she wants sex with me? I haven't had a girlfriend yet.

A There's a big gap between fancying someone and asking them to go to bed with you. The gap is usually filled with getting to know them, confirming that you like them, finding out how much they like you, becoming attached to them, even falling in love. Fancying begins with sexual attraction but human beings don't usually feel safe mating with relative strangers. We think you are full of strong sexual desires which take over a little but this is a normal aspect of puberty. P.S. When you've finished staring, why not offer to buy her an ice cream?

Q My boyfriend asked if I masturbate and I felt a fool because I don't know how to. How old should you be to do it?

A There are no ages, and there are no 'shoulds'. You can masturbate at any time of life, or not, depending on your feelings and beliefs. There are some women who *never* masturbate because they didn't discover it before marriage and possibly don't feel the need afterwards. Other women first played with their genitals during childhood while many only experiment in their teens. Women tend to do it later, and less, than men, partly because their genitals are recessed, not 'to hand', and partly because of sexist double standards suggesting that what is normal for a boy is dirty for a girl. George Bernard Shaw said 'Ninety-nine per cent of people masturbate and one per cent are liars' but we think he was generalizing about men.

Q **All the other boys have bigger penises than mine and some of them even say they have sex. I'm worried because mine doesn't seem to have changed (groan). I am nearly 14.**

A Since the average human vagina is only *four inches long*, by how much do you wish your penis to exceed such capacity? If you complain we are missing the point (and we do believe that sex is not just about intercourse), tell us what you want the extra inches for. Impressing your friends? Frightening females? Seriously, stop telling yourself you *are* a cock. From what you've said, it seems you've entered puberty later than your schoolfriends. This feels basically miserable but it isn't a physical mistake. Within the next year to 18 months, your development will occur, and first to grow will be the item in question. Some of your friends seem disproportionately big only because they have adult-sized penises on boy-sized bodies.

Q **My penis is covered with little white pimples. I've never had sex but I'm scared I've got VD. I can't ask my mum and dad. What should I do?**

A Relax for a start. It's pretty difficult to catch a 'sex disease' while still a virgin. Secondly, these pimples are almost certainly the oily sebaceous glands that develop as part of the physical changes of puberty. Their job is to keep your new pubic hairs in good condition. They especially stand out if you stretch the penile or scrotal skin, and boys often first notice them during masturbation. Don't they?

Q My boobs flop up and down when I play volleyball but my mother won't let me have a bra. All the boys in school make fun of me – what can I do?

A Demonstrate the problem, either by running up and down on the spot, or by asking your mother to come and watch you at school. If paying for the bra is an issue, offer to find the cash yourself from the proceeds of birthdays or some Saturday job. If all else fails, corner a favourite female teacher, unload the problem on her and plead with her to tackle your mum. Whether there is a real need (because your breasts are weighty) or quite simply because *you* would *feel* better in a bra, you ought to be able to get one.

Q Help! After reading a sex education book I've tried to find my clitoris but it doesn't seem to be there.

A It is, but may be hidden in the upper folds of your pubis. Size may also vary from a few millimetres to a couple of centimetres. (We suspect that the claimed record of twelve *inches* is a printing error since hardly any penises amount to 10 inches.) Go to bed with a good torch, a mirror and a clear idea of the upper central location of the human clitoris and probe your folds. It may be well-covered by 'foreskin' or fleshy adipose. Moderate stroking of the region might help you pinpoint the exact focus of delight and there you'll find the object of your search.

Q **I'm 15 and completely flat-chested. The other girls call me 'George'. Nobody will ever fancy me looking like this.**

A Not true at all. First, it could be that *all* your development is running later than others in your class at school. Breasts can only grow under the influence of female hormones and you don't get your supply *until* the first part of puberty. Puberty may commence at any age between extremes of 9 and 17. Second, it's perfectly normal to have 'smaller' breasts, especially if that's part of your family's body-shape. So take a deep breath and appraise the appearance of your mother, aunts and sisters. Ask them about their teenage development. Third, size of boob does not affect breast-feeding. Some of the best breast-feeders have been 'flat-chested'. Fourth, boob-size *does* affect the supply of boyfriends, but not in the way you suppose. Girls with huge breasts often attract immature men. They certainly attract unwelcome abuse. They often begin to feel exploited. Making love may be uncomfortable because heavy mammaries tend to pull at the hair on a boy's chest. By contrast, many males enjoy the less obvious look of a girl with a delicate, elegant shape. Fifth, your real problem is wanting a boyfriend and you're blaming your poor old bust for his absence. Isn't that two scapegoats for the price of one?

Q I'm 13 and believe nobody likes me. I've actually been all the way with a boy now and he still doesn't like me.

A So now you've learned that even having sex with boys is not enough to buy you friendship. Obviously, it is horrible to think nobody likes you. But try to compare notes with girlfriends. Work out how your family behaved differently from theirs. See how you've actually been given a pretty low opinion of yourself by some of those closest to you. It's probably because you haven't been surrounded by friendly people at home, perhaps having to 'bargain' for their attention, that you've come unstuck in the world outside. You don't quite know how to make friendship 'boundaries' work. Certainly, we suggest you don't sleep with a boy unless you first know two things about him: 1. His family story, way of life, and reasons for liking you. 2. His ability to meet *your* emotional needs.

Q I'm 18 and have recently taken my relationship with my partner into a sexual dimension. The second time, all was going well when I lost my erection. The problem is the condom. Putting this on interferes with my sexual momentum and destroys spontaneity.

A It really needn't. All you have to do is make the donning of the condom a natural and exciting part of foreplay. So when you've undressed, and she's kissed your chest, and you've stroked her buttocks, and hands begin to sneak towards genitals, get her to roll the friendly rubber sheath *slowly* down your penis, alternately teasing you and pinching your penis head (so you don't come too quickly). Allow her to spend *several minutes* happily playing with you. After the first few seconds, we suspect you'll begin to forget you're even wearing the thing, so much will pleasure rule your thoughts. Subtle hint: unwrap the condom and place it somewhere handy under the bed before you get undressed (and look at the question on page 34).

Q My best friend and I both love the same boy. I know he prefers me but I'm afraid to do anything in case my best friend gets angry.

A We guess you are just becoming ready to start opposite sex relationships. Perhaps you've been going round in a crowd of girls for quite a while. This is natural, but it's equally natural one day to break out. It can feel painful, even scary, to kiss goodbye to any phase of your life and this feeling may affect the present situation, erupting as guilt. You're not quite sure it's a good idea to give up the security of an all-girl friendship, but you do know deep inside that you want the man. However, it does not have to be simply either/or. There's nothing you can do about him preferring *you*, or about your friend getting furious, but you could certainly stay in touch with her, offering to go double-dating sometimes when she's found a new boyfriend too.

Q I'm 17 and haven't started shaving yet. I have no hair on my chest either. Should I see my doctor?

A Your doctor would always be happy to see you when you're worried. But hairiness is a genetic lottery, depending on race, family and luck. If both parents are 'hirsute', you are likely to be hairy too, but it's not inevitable. Further, even if your father has hair on his *back*, he may not have needed to begin shaving his *chin* until he was 20. Individual development during puberty is extremely varied. Chest hair too may first begin to show at about the age of 12, but not finish spreading until the early 20s, or even later. Hair on the ears, on moles, on the back of the neck, eyebrows and nostrils *continues* to get more widespread and wiry in the *middle* years.

Q **I am 16 years old and madly in love. He's nearly six feet tall and very popular, but there's a problem. I'm too shy to ask him out.**

A It's not your fault if you've been brought up shyly. Either you've learned to avoid trouble at home by keeping quiet, or in your family very few words were needed by people to make themselves understood. The sensible thing is to accept that when going beyond your circle you may need a different type of skill, language and behaviour.

Shy people have very 'stiff' faces. They don't use the muscles of their eyes, mouths or foreheads very much when talking or (above all) listening. The major problem is that by keeping their heads down, their voices low, their eyes away from others and their faces frozen into a mask *they don't appear shy but cold.* One very good way to loosen up is take your face for a 'jog'. What you do is sit in front of a mirror and practise saying 'me/you/me/you/me/you/me/you' quite loud, lots of times over, to get those facial muscles working. Also practise doing ultra-slow exaggerated smiles as another muscle exercise. Then try getting a spark in encounters that are not matters of great emotional importance – like dialling directory enquiries or travel information on the telephone and seeing if you can make some friendly remarks, or bantering with your neighbourhood grocer. What we are saying is that shyness needs a *general* approach.

Once you build up your overall confidence (and this can happen quite quickly), then you can take a fresh self to the man of your choice and let him know there's a new woman in town. At the very least, you will be able to breathe (not choke), smile (not scowl), listen (not panic) and talk (not clam up).

That's a remarkable start.

Q **Some girls at school a year younger than me have already started sleeping with their boyfriends and I haven't. I haven't wanted to, but I feel backward.**

A Starting too early can make you accident-prone (pregnancy, cervical disease and a broken heart). Starting in later teens frankly holds fewer problems. As you grow more mature, the chances are you have greater social skill and judgement to manage the encounter to your advantage. Instead of losing the 'competition' (as you see it) you could actually win the game.

Q **I'm a fat 14-year-old boy and everyone makes fun of me. But I want a girlfriend. Do fat boys ever get girls?**

A Yes, all the time, though fat *men* will probably find it easier than fat boys. Down the ages and even today, fat has been associated in the minds of some women with power and success. Then again there are those who prefer a man who won't deny himself a second piece of strawberry cheesecake on the grounds that perhaps he won't deny them the same, or similar indulgences.

It's obviously in your medical interest not to be overweight. However, there is a good chance that if you eat moderately in your mid-to-late teens, much of the childhood fat will disappear. But one word of warning. If you become svelte and trim, you will probably want to pay the world back for its earlier unkindnesses. Breaking women's hearts may seem like sweet revenge. But be aware of the inner damage the teasing will have caused. One day you'll need to deal with this directly and talking about it might prove safer than wrecking lives. P.S. – don't crash-diet, or fad-diet. They never work in the long run.

Q I took home this girl who said I could have sex with her. Then she passed out dead drunk. I don't much like her but I was *very* devastated when I couldn't make love to her even though she was completely at my mercy. Why?

A Why was she silly enough to ask you? Why couldn't you do it? Or why did you even try? Whatever your question, the answer must cope with your super-masculine assumptions. First, do you really have to copulate on demand? Just because the opportunity is available? Second, do you really feel compelled to go to bed with a girl you don't fancy? Simply because, like Mount Everest, she is there? Third, do you really regard making love to an unconscious body exciting or does the potential pleasure result from feeling freer of anxiety? You say you 'had her at your mercy'. Has sex always been such a dreadful battle for you? And fourth, are you always so tough on your body (and mind) that you see them as tools (or weapons) to be used at will? If so, we have news for you. Your central nervous system is not The Pentagon, and won't play war. Male sexual circuitry is actually designed to prevent erection in the absence of positive desire. This was no 'failure'. You simply had no feelings.

Q I'm a 17-year-old girl with several friends who are boys. I've been to bed with two of them but without changing the friendships in any way. I felt fine about this but my girlfriend said she didn't understand how I could remain so cool.

A We're sure you like your lovers a lot (and this is a totally different problem from the previous question). You are simply reserving the right to be sexual even though you are not romantically 'in love' with the two men concerned. Some people feel like this; others couldn't do it. So far sex for you has been an extension of the bonds of friendship. None of this means that you will escape falling in love eventually. But nor does it mean you are an emotional cripple. Learn to assess your girlfriend as an individual whose pattern of needs is different from your own.

Q I got very passionate with my girlfriend last night and told her I loved her. Today her bunch of friends giggle every time they see me. Surely she wouldn't have told them my secret, would she?

A Your girlfriend knows the answer, and perhaps her mates. You need to confront her, explaining very clearly that if she is someone who is going to make private communications public, then she's not the girl you thought she was. Naturally, this would make you think twice before trusting her again. Please don't feel ashamed of expressing your love. The giggles simply mean you're more grown up than the audience.

Q I got totally out of control with my boyfriend last night and our clothes all ended up on the sitting-room floor. We only stopped at the last minute because the door-bell rang (we didn't answer it). I don't think I'll be able to stop next time. I want him inside me so much.

A If you really feel you are likely to have intercourse soon (and your feelings have convinced this jury that it's probable), then tell your doctor or family planning clinic you need some advice about contraception. However, once you've obtained contraception, don't think you are *compelled* to have intercourse. The choice is still to be made, just as it was before.

Q I am 18 and my girlfriend is 15. We are both virgins. I want to have sex, but my girlfriend says no. But if you don't make it with your partner how can you show love? We agreed nothing should happen till we both wanted it. But we've been together for four months and I'm ready now.

A But she is not, and the three-year difference in your ages may well be proving decisive. We suspect you are both 'virginity anxious' – you to lose it, she to keep it. You both seem concerned about 'proofs' of love. You think love means saying yes. She thinks love means not bothering her, and she protects herself with the deal you both agreed. In fact, love is not about power or making people do things. That's why your relationship is not yet good enough to be sexual. So it's not your wishes that can be faulted, but your understanding. If you wish to have sex today, now, at this minute, then it cannot be with her. You must move on. But if you would like to know how to express love and to see what sexual reward it can ultimately bring, then tell her you can see her point of view, explain your anxiety, describe your frustration and show her in words, kisses, sighs and looks how much you continue to care about her. Do this for long enough and she will feel she can trust you all the way.

Q I'm mad about this sexy boy but when we went out he constantly touched my breasts and tried to get his hand under my clothes. I want to be seen with him and talk with him but ended up rejecting him. How could I get him to go slower?

A By rejecting behaviour you don't want while explaining your motives, just as you have to us. Perhaps he feels obliged to come on like a stallion since he believes this is what a girl expects? If so, educate him. Make it clear you welcome sensuous behaviour *gradually*, after a few dates. You could even tell him you would start complaining if after weeks together he hadn't touched you at all!

Q I'm so embarrassed because I get erections in public. I just can't control my thoughts or my penis and I'm sure all the world can see.

A When during teenage your body is bathed in sex hormones, in concentrations to which you are not used, there is no mystery as to why your penis rises. You literally cannot help it. The new baggier fashions in trousers will hide most of the results but tell yourself that what's in your mind cannot be in everybody else's. For the most part, people think about themselves rather than others and many wouldn't notice if you had a permanent erection. Of those who do, however, most would rather not draw attention to your condition for obvious reasons – while the rest may simply enjoy the thought. Some women do feel intrigued by male arousal, just as you enjoy the thought of watching a woman's nipples become erect beneath her braless blouse.

Q When I try to masturbate, my foreskin hurts. It doesn't seem to retract far enough.

A But does it prevent full erection or not? If it does, you have phimosis (a too-tight foreskin) and the doctor may recommend a simple snip, or full circumcision (very routine and pain-free). If it does not, you could have adhesions between penis-crown and foreskin or a foreskin that has never been stretched. Either way, remember that it's not absolutely essential to retract this tissue of skin for purposes of sex. Should you wish to ease it, use baby oil as a lubricant and roll the overlayer downwards with the gentlest of pressures, a little further each time.

Q My boyfriend and I got carried away and covered in lovebites. My dad says I'm a whore but I've never had intercourse.

A Your father sounds jealous as well as obnoxious, but if keeping the peace at home is important for a few more years ask your boyfriend to confine his lovebites to your less public regions.

Q This boy talked me into letting him have sex when I didn't want to and next day his friend came and tried to do the same, saying as I'd done it for one, I'd do it for the other. I was a bit drunk then, and I don't know how I'll ever face my friends again.

A Let she that is without sin cast the first stone . . . We are all prone to make mistakes (thank goodness because otherwise we'd never learn a thing). Tell yourself, and others if necessary, that this was an error of judgement on your part. For just a minute, you believed this young man was worth having.

Q I'm 19, have been in my first sexual relationship for two years but can now see it's not going to last, certainly not for a lifetime. How do I start again, knowing I might run the risk of contracting AIDS?

A As more heterosexuals acquire HIV, this is going to be one of the big dilemmas over the next 15 years. Your bitter choice (which the older generation uniformly feels sad and guilty about, though that's small consolation) is between celibacy on the one hand, and trying to minimize the risks on the other. If sex is to remain part of your life, then you have to pick lovers carefully, get to know their background before exploring their bodies, consider the pros and cons of HIV-testing, use condoms and avoid high risk behaviour (including unguarded sex with extra partners). In the early days of a relationship, it is prudent to avoid penetration, preferring mutual masturbation, unless and until you are sure the man is going to become a regular boyfriend. This is in his interest every bit as much as yours. If he complains, quote this slogan: 'They used to say masturbation could kill you. Now they say it could save your life'.

Q How do you make love without having intercourse?

A You can kiss, caress and stroke your partner's entire body. You can indulge in pillow talk, romantic or lecherous to taste. You can shower in tee shirts, use wet ice cubes as a tease, use perfumes to intoxicate, inhale each other's sex musks, wear masks, make jokes, you can blow on wetted areas of skin, play master and slave or mistress and creature, dress in super-skins of silk, satin, rubber, leather or lace, you can cross-dress or wear make-up, you can watch in mirrors or look at pictorial erotica. All this is available as preliminary enhancement if you keep an open mind.

Thereafter, if you want an orgasm you can use any of the extra penetrative sites of the human body (hands, armpits, elbows, toes, knees, thighs, breasts, chest) for him, and the more prominent parts of male anatomy for her (fingers, hands, arms, knees, legs, nose, toes, elbows, hips, chin). Either sex may simply be gratified by use of a vibrator (best for him on underside of penis head, and the perineum. For her, on or around the clitoris but not inserted unless she claims 'G-Spot' sensitivity). Most commonly, of course, you will let your fingers do the talking but do ask to be shown by your partner how they like to do it to themselves so you can copy and learn. Also look at a book like *Massage and Loving* by Anne Hooper.

Q I love girls, I just can't help myself. But the girls always seem to think the words 'I love you' imply some kind of exclusive commitment. I'm always in trouble because just after orgasm I tell them I love them.

A The need to express love after intercourse is often the need to say how wonderful and grateful you feel, or how much you like sex itself. Why not rephrase your post-coital appreciation along such lines as 'that was great' or 'you're marvellous' or 'I'm so happy'? Then your partner could neither take offence nor feel misled.

Q My friend has only petted with her boyfriend but has missed two periods and fears she's pregnant. Could this happen without intercourse?

A All too easily and in this sense 'virgin birth' is commonplace. Her boyfriend has ejaculated or leaked somewhere near her vagina, and in the moist steamy conditions of mutual arousal a determined sperm has possibly wriggled its way across the intervening space and into her birth canal. She should see her doctor at once.

Q I think my friend must be pregnant but she seems to be in a dream about it. All that bothers her is that her boyfriend doesn't want to make love anymore. How can I get her to wake up?

A In surveys of late abortion, the majority of women were very young, mostly still at school and they had 'dealt' with pregnancy by denying it. In the end, bodily changes alone forced them to see what was going to happen. It sounds as if your friend may be among these and for her health's sake she does indeed need to wake up. Even if it means risking a row, try to talk to her about it. Obviously, you will have to listen to her emotional problems too, about her sense of loss concerning the father of her child who seems to have grown physically cold. But having done that, raise what's on your mind. Take her to the clinic. Whether she's going to have a termination or keep the child, she needs medical checking now. Both abortion and pregnancy have their risks and the sooner these are planned for the better.

Q I'm a 19-year-old man. I recently met and went to bed with the daughter of an old family friend. I thought she was my age but afterwards she revealed she was only 15 and could have me sent to prison for illegal sex. She keeps ringing and asking for things, including more sex and money.

A Although you are technically and legally in the wrong, blackmail is also a crime. We suggest you tape-record this young woman's demands, then use the evidence to negotiate a truce or defend yourself in court as necessary. Meanwhile, learn from experience that a woman may be younger than she looks.

Q I am a 19-year-old girl who has fallen in love with a 38-year-old friend of my father's. We are both in love but my father would die if he knew.

A All teenagers need to separate from their parents, transferring their love to people beyond the family group. Without being ageist about this, the natural process does appear to have wobbled in your case since your lover is old enough to be your parent. 'So what?', you may say. 'So is there a why?', we reply. If there is an underlying reason, it only matters that you should know about it. After all, you don't want to be confused by unrealistic expectations or programmed by family assumptions. You want to be yourself.

Think about the 'script' you've been asked to learn. Have you been cast as 'Daddy's Girl', with a firm direction never to become independent? Have you been paternally dominated, practically becoming terrified to speak out of turn? Have you felt deprived of good fathering, so much so that you need to make up for what you've missed? And how will any of this affect the relationship with your father's friend? Do you feel as if one person in this affair has to do all the controlling? If so, we think you are going to run into trouble. Whatever is going on, you are certainly old enough at 19 to pick your own friends and lovers, but think about the questions we have raised. If your father has problems with your love life that's his responsibility and, while he may be angrily jealous, he's unlikely to drop dead. Maybe part of your growing up is to stop living in awe of his feelings?

Q My boyfriend has left me after a passionate year together for someone with half the brain and twice the boobs. How could he do it? I'm 16 and he's 18.

A He could well have made a mistake, but that's his problem now, not yours. Perhaps he was saying he wanted to alter the balance in the relationship – your fear seems to be that he wanted less intellectual action and a lot more upfront sex – but we don't know. People go through rapid changes of inclination in their late teens. Emotionally, perhaps it was the right time for him to move on, although a disaster for you. You need to mourn what you have lost; to register the sadness of what has passed. Talk privately to his photograph, whether you speak words of love or hate, and let your friends know how upset you're feeling.

Q I'm a 16-year-old girl with a passionate crush on my (female) art teacher. I can't tell anyone about this because my mum never understands my feelings.

A And that's one very good reason why you have now fallen in love. It's because you feel emotionally distant from your family that your 'psychic radar' has homed in on your art teacher as a substitute. We know you find her very attractive but are equally sure she is one who has seemed kind and considerate of your feelings as well. In short, she is an 'adopted mother' as well as a wished-for lover. There's absolutely nothing wrong in modelling yourself on an older woman whom you love and admire. The feelings are real. They simply have this extra dimension because you have no other good maternal relationship. If you have a school counsellor, try to talk about things there. But we guess you need to be in love like this as a way of getting through the next few months. Remember that most teachers have had pupils fall for them and they do realize what goes on, and why.

Q My mother keeps asking when I'm going to get a boyfriend (I'm 18) and I keep putting off telling her. How do you tell your mother you are gay?

A The answer depends on your mother. If you're convinced she's the sort of person who'd say 'do not darken my doors again', you may *never* want to tell her out of sensible self-interest. If your mother is reasonably open, you may decide to go ahead but choosing time, place, and circumstance carefully. For intance, ensure when you talk she is neither tired, angry, busy nor hungry. Even then, pick your words. Instead of bleakly announcing 'I am a lesbian', say 'I've fallen in love with a friend who happens to be a woman'. For all the sad stories of children being disowned, the majority of parents are eventually supportive. One heartening tale comes from a family where the mother replied 'as a matter of fact, there have been times when I thought I was one too.'

Q My parents divorced five years ago and since that time my mother must have had 20 lovers. I'm always finding her in bed with someone or other and our house resembles a bus station. I am worried it will make me promiscuous too.

A You may simply feel worried full stop. The uncertainty created by this situation must be confusing for you. But one of the sad facts of divorce is that the family can never be the same afterwards and your mother's behaviour seems to have settled into a pattern. What you really need is an area of peace, stability and privacy. Put a lock on the door of your room so you feel secure in there. Work out a sensible routine for the time you spend in the house so you can make life more predictable. Tell your mother about your distress so that even if she carries on as before, she might consider not disturbing you so much, or making you meet *all* her friends. Other options would include going to live with your father if he can have you. As for your potential promiscuity, this experience is as likely to make you monogamous as polygamous. In other words, the whole situation is making you anxious but *you* remain in charge of your future love life. That hasn't changed.

Q The other day my dad came into my room (I am 18) and said 'Have you anything to tell me?' I replied no. He repeated the question, then said 'Are you one of them?' When I admitted I was gay, he said 'Where did we go wrong?' and 'Why are you doing this to us?' I still don't know what to tell him.

A You will probably have to tell your father that he has done absolutely nothing 'wrong'. Nor are you 'doing this to them'. You simply *are* homosexual. Your parents may not like it, but your sexual identity is neither defiance nor disaster. It simply closes down some options, which may make them feel sad, while opening up others. There is often no obvious 'cause' of a sexual orientation, gay or straight. It's more like a lifetime's evolution of tastes for which there is no scientific accounting. Why do some parents like comedy on TV, old dance-band music, root beer and heavily-embossed wallpaper? These questions are more trivial but the answers are equally hard to find. Be patient as your parents come to terms with this.

Q I have been brought up in a one-parent family by my mother who is still quite young and we often do things together. Now a new manfriend seems to be preferring me to her and I can see she is eaten up with bad feeling. I can't handle this.

A Well, when all is said and done she is your mother, not your sister. It sounds as if she has the roles confused and maybe you do too. If the man is *her* friend, in *her* age group, we suggest you bow out. If, on the other hand, he is of your generation, and you say he prefers you, why should you give him up? Your mother seems to feel competitive with you and however super a person she is, needs to get on with her own life and allow you to fashion yours. Try putting more distance into the relationship for both your sakes.

Q My parents are too bloody liberal. They told my girlfriend last night that she was welcome to be 'private' with me in their house any time. The implication was definitely to do what they call 'screwing'. They make me sick. My girlfriend was extremely embarrassed since we haven't got anywhere near that stage yet. How can I control them?

A Perhaps by explaining to them, as you have to us, that their 'over-the-top', slightly 60s approach, has impeded your sex life rather than enhanced it. The generations often fail to understand each other so it would be most helpful to define your problems in their sexual terms.

Part two: Parents' questions

Q **My teenage daughter looks at me with such horror when I cuddle her father that it's making me self-conscious. Is it wrong to do this now she's older?**

A On the contrary, she needs a good example of physical closeness as a normal part of life. Her embarrassment shows she is trying to bridge the gap between child and adult, parent and person. This learning is absolutely vital. If you stopped, what sort of message would she receive?

Q **My 14-year-old son is incredibly prudish. He's shocked by topless pin-ups, bad language and tells us off if we crack a saucy joke or laugh suggestively. What's happened?**

A You almost said, 'Where have we gone wrong?', and the answer is that children get influenced by many people besides their parents. Think about it. Do their grandparents hold these opinions? Or teachers? Or preachers? Or TV evangelists? Or other mentors or friends? Or does it come from books? You must also think about your own beliefs. Have you tried to ram 'permissiveness' down your child's throat with the predictable response that he is 'rebelling' against your values?

Q **My 14-year-old son seems extraordinarily interested in girls. Surely he's too young?**

A You may not have noticed, but children grow up earlier than they did even ten years ago. Some girls are starting their periods at 9 and 10 (each decade the average age of onset falls by one month) and both sexes are fashion-conscious by this stage. Then again, the age of consent for sex and marriage in English-speaking countries was as low as 12 in 1880. So do you really think your son's behaviour all that strange? Get to know him better.

Q **My 13-year-old daughter still comes to bed with us for a cuddle in the morning. I think she is too old for this now but my husband disagrees. Am I wrong?**

A You are right. Girls generally reach sexual maturity two years earlier than boys and 13 is the average age for the commencement of menstruation. At this point, your daughter is rapidly becoming a sexual adult and it is no longer appropriate for her to have such confusing bodily contact with her father in the marital bed. We don't mean you should start a touching taboo – just keep it out of suggestive locations in nightclothes.

Q My 16-year-old son continues to show absolutely no interest in the opposite sex at all. Should I be worried?

A We take it you mean he shows no 'interest' in the same sex either, and that you are specifically concerned about his enthusiasm for heterosexual romance? We suggest you are still jumping the gun. Your concern might be justified in three or four years' time but it will always be his battle, not yours, since you cannot arrange for him to have your feelings. (Even if his inclinations are gay, these may not be focused for many months ahead).

Q I'm the mother of a 14-year-old daughter who unashamedly undresses in front of me still. Is it wrong to be embarrassed?

A It can't be wrong but it does go to show that you are far more aware of your daughter's burgeoning sexuality than she is. You are also bothered by it. However, you must have done something right to bring up a daughter with fewer inhibitions than you have.

Q I found a condom in my 14-year-old daughter's pocket. What should I do?

A Perhaps first of all breathe a sigh of relief that if she is precocious enough to be sexually active, she is also precocious enough to protect herself from pregnancy – you hope. But of course it is never safe to make assumptions. As her legal guardian, as well as her friend, you need to know what, if anything, is going on. Choose a good time to talk calmly, then tell her what you've found.

Even if she says she was given it in the school playground, use the opportunity to discuss what condoms are for and why they are thought to be a good idea. This might let you hear what she thinks about the subject of sleeping with boyfriends. If she turns out to be sleeping with hers, you need to know more before taking decisions. What sort of guy is he? Is this a steady relationship (even at 14), or a passing fancy? Can she deal with it, or is she under heavy pressure? Is she defiant and blasé, or do you see her, possibly for the first time, as very grown up? Does she seem to be using her relationship as compensation in some way, or is it sweetly loving? In effect, is she crying for help or not? When you've got these answers you'll know what you need to do. Please remember that some teenagers are mature beyond their years. Think about the consequences of any laws you may lay down. A negotiated compromise to which all parties agree might be your best outcome – you know, 'wait a while but not forever'.

Q **Our family is extrovert and open but my son has just been banned from his girlfriend's house for always hugging and kissing her. Are we at fault?**

A It is valuable to be able to use touch to express feelings so never regret teaching your son this lesson. However he has just learned that not everyone can tolerate the same openness. It might have been a good idea to let him know that different families have different rules of affectionate conduct. However, it won't kill him to absorb this information today, and you can make *her* especially welcome in your home.

Q **I think my 17-year-old son may be homosexual. Should I tell him I suspect?**

A Unless you've got a special reason leading you to suppose your son may come to harm it would be better to leave any revelations up to him. First, he may not feel ready to talk about this yet. Second, there is presumably a chance that you've got it wrong on what could be a very sensitive subject for him. What you could do constructively is show by the way you talk about homosexuals and sexual identity that you are not a rejecting person while also confirming from time to time how much you love him.

Q **My 17-year-old daughter always seems to be hugging her schoolfriend. Does this mean she's a lesbian?**

A Probably not, since women have always been permitted to behave more demonstrably together than (Anglo-Saxon) men. There are phases in adolescence when girls become so involved with their friends that they quite literally can't leave them alone. A minority of girls may turn this into something erotic, or para-sexual. Yet it may still be mainly a friendship 'frenzy'. Although some lesbian women are aware of their sexual identity early in life, others don't find it out until their 20s and 30s. If you think the kids are going too far, you might say '*I* understand it, but others may not', though we still get the feeling that the discomfort is primarily *yours*.

Q **Can you cure a child of homosexuality?**

A No, because it is not a disease and for more than a decade now the governing body of US psychiatry has concluded for its members that homosexuality is indicative of no type of 'pathology'. In the 50s and 60s, however, the story was different, and punitive psychologists were prepared to offer 'aversion therapy' as a serious cure. However, this treatment made homosexual arousal painful rather than converting gays into straights. One homosexual whom doctors attempted to convert was made to drink salt water every time he had a gay fantasy. The only result was that he became seasick.

Q **I found my 18-year-old on the sofa having sex with his girlfriend. Was I right to be angry?**

A That depends on your background and morality. If you have been conditioned to think this sort of behaviour sinful, unethical or bad mannered, it's no surprise that you lost your cool. If the vision raised uncomfortable sexual feelings too – perhaps of jealousy or envy, even lust – then you might well experience rage to cope with them. Possibly you felt territorial? 'How dare they invade my relaxation space with their condoms and love stains?' We can appreciate how you might react. But the important question is what you are going to do next, because whatever has happened to you, there are two young people who are now feeling rather embarrassed and distressed? Could you let them realize what a shock you got and gently suggest that you do understand their need to love, even though family living rooms make inadequate boudoirs?

Q **My neighbour saw my 17-year-old son coming out of a massage parlour recently. Why on earth would he want to go to such a place?**

A To gain sexual experience, to satisfy his curiosity, even to go 'slumming'. It is historically common for men to choose to pay for sex on the first few occasions because they are dying to discover what it's about long before they may be able to sustain an intimate relationship. If you really dislike what he's done, then try revving up his rate of *social* activity (although not quite as blatantly as the parents in the movie *The Graduate* which you might watch with some profit).

Q **My teenage daughter is depressed after an abortion. What can she do?**

A Nothing in a hurry. She has got to sail through an ocean of sad feelings. You can help by talking about a life that might have been and a future she couldn't make happen. She may also have difficult thoughts about the man who made her pregnant, about her inability to avoid tough choices, together with thoughts about any other major past losses which this event will almost inevitably recall. It may also be a good move to suggest she talks things over with a professional counsellor, many of whom now offer a special service in relation to abortion.

Q **Is it true there are special health risks for a teenager who is sexually active?**

A There appears to be a greater chance of teenagers acquiring herpes or genital warts and the youthful cervix is apparently more vulnerable to viral attack than that of the fully mature female. Both herpes and warts, therefore, involve an increased long-term risk of uterine cancer. If either is contracted, six-monthly cervical smears should be taken.

Q **My 16-year-old daughter dresses like a tart. She knows this upsets me but refuses to change.**

A Your daughter, like any other adolescent, is trying to find her own personal style, sexual and otherwise. She may be getting this a little wrong, perhaps over the top, but sometimes we feel we can only learn by taking things to extremes. At least, she can feel, comfortably sure she's found a fashion identity that you'd never be seen dead in, so in her terms she's successfully 'created a new person separate from Mum'. But further, she seems to be on the one hand attractive, and on the other dramatic. This probably means there is a part of her which feels the opposite – less attractive and not very significant.

Confidence is a fragile plant at the best of times and thoughtless parents can easily destroy it. If you could congratulate her when she pleases you but remain mute when you think she's got it wrong, you will do more to help her form sensible judgements than if you constantly nag. Revealing her panties like a tart may be a misguided method of proving oneself sexually attractive, and therefore lovable, but she has to discover for herself that loveability does not come from sexual *availability*. Your tragedy is that if you tell her how to live you'll destroy her capacity to do so.

Q My son has taken to spending hours in the bathroom. I suspect from the evidence that he is masturbating. Should I say anything?

A No, that would be rude, unless you or the family need to use the room and can't because the door is always locked. If this is your only bathroom, we suggest you ask him not to occupy the chamber during rush hour(s).

Q My 16-year-old's idea of a cuddle is to press his whole body against me. I want to hug him back, but will he get the wrong idea?

A Sons need cuddles from their mothers at most ages, although some respond more demonstratively than others. However, when they start seeing women as sex objects, in early teenage, you should begin to alter the way in which cuddles are received. If he presses his whole body against yours, move slightly sideways to avoid his full frontal. Begin the habit of putting an arm round his shoulder and hugging him from the side. A goodbye hug and kiss can still be managed with heads and shoulders pressed close but other regions held apart. He'll pick up the message which is quite a good one to hear – that you now acknowledge his sexual status while continuing to offer him your complete affection.

Q **My daughter has a new boyfriend every month and this worries me. Will she ever settle down?**

A You can console yourself with the thought that practically everyone who can be married does get married. They may not stay with the same person for life, and they may not be married when you want them to be, but the human race still strives after this estate. Perhaps your daughter is checking out all the possibilities because she knows how important it is to pick a winner? Or more subtly, perhaps she realizes she must work through a lot of personal experiences before being able to offer a man a mature partnership? If she shows genuine signs of depression or self-dislike, the problem is different and you could try to probe the wound – otherwise surgery is not called for. Would you worry so much if she were a son?

Q **I'd like my kids to think that the best sexual relationships are built on love. Am I hideously old-fashioned?**

A You are romantically acknowledging the special quality possessed by loving relationships which become sexual. But there are many fine unions based on different assumptions. The relationship that is poignant when 'ships pass in the night', perhaps in wartime. The relationship which is pure comedy. One based on friendship where flirtation flares into passion. Another when colleagues at work fall into each other's arms after a campaign triumph. One based on curiosity, when a teenager needs to know 'what it will be like', and many more – all these can be excellent sexual experiences in their own right.

Q I have read my daughter's diary and she is having an affair with a married man. She is not yet 18. Should I intervene?

A If your daughter wanted you to know about the affair she would have confided in you. If she is otherwise behaving normally, we would think it important to respect her privacy, independence and even her 'right to make possible mistakes'. A 17-year-old is a virtual adult and needs to be recognized as such. The fact that you are reading her diary shows you have not so far done this. The only time to interfere would be if she were obviously distressed and needing help.

6 Mid-life crisis?

Q **Is there a male *sexual* menopause?**

A No. Men do not 'reach a date' after which they become uniformly infertile and their bodies cease to produce sex hormones. What happens instead is that after about the age of 40, they may find it takes longer to *get* an adequate erection. It may take more stimulation of the penis to *keep* an adequate erection. The degree of firmness of erection may decrease. It may be more difficult to *regain* an erection once lost. It may become more difficult to ejaculate. The sensation of orgasm may tend to decrease. The expulsive power of ejaculation may tend to decline. The 'refractory' period between orgasms will almost certainly increase in duration. And the overall level of sexual desire may decline.

These apart, sex retains its potential for bliss. The best way to minimize these effects is to continue to express your sexual needs *regularly*. Bodily systems that aren't used tend to become use-less – 'Go to work on an orgasm!' You also need to educate your partner to these potential changes so that during foreplay she gives your penis more handwork and maintains this contact right up to the moment of penetration.

Q **Is there a male menopause anyway?**

A Yes, men go through a change of life emotionally just like women. They have to come to terms with age, loss of youthful looks and the feeling that they cannot control life. Put one way, they need to acquire a new set of ideas to suit reality. They may have to agree to settle for less promotion at work and less personal stress since they have passed their physical performance peaks. Put another way, they have to abandon dreams of 'who they might have been' as workers or lovers. They need to develop a new self-image. This can be intensely painful for all concerned, including family, since the experience may be depressive or aggressive.

Some men take to their beds. Others dye their hair and date their dollies. Strategies include denial ('I can still outdrink, outwalk, outscrew anyone') to projecting the distress onto others ('It is all your fault I've never become a film star/Nobel Prize Winner'). Look out for special trouble if previous 'life changes' were mismanaged. The man for whom adolescence was hell will have acquired few skills to cope in *any* identity crisis. He will also re-experience some of his suppressed youthful pains. Bear this in mind when you see your husband and teenage son competing to appraise themselves in the bathroom mirror – one to see if his beard is beginning to whiten, the other for signs of its first growth. Their confusions are similar.

Q **I've been told women go off sex when they reach the menopause. Is this true?**

A Those who do are mainly influenced by the folklore prejudice that sex is restricted to the young and fertile. Some women find that loss of oestrogen and progesterone does make them lose desire but most abstainers are suffering from loss of confidence rather than hormones. The best preventive is to maintain regular sexual routines throughout your 40s. Note that while hormone replacement therapy may help with deficiencies of vaginal lubrication and other symptoms it is not a patent aphrodisiac.

Q **I've heard a woman's sex life can improve after the menopause.**

A Life can indeed become more erotic because you no longer have to worry about pregnancy (provided you've gone two years without a period). Many also feel cheery because they have fewer childcare and financial constraints after 50.

Q **I'm 50 and I've never had an orgasm. Am I too old to start?**

A Absolutely not – many women of your age climax for the first time when they learn self-pleasuring techniques. A vibrator is also invaluable.

Q **Are vibrators dangerous?**

A No. People are. Vibrators used according to the manufacturers' instructions are as safe as any other hand-held electrical appliance.

Q **I live in dread of the day that my wife's periods stop, for she has said that this is when sexual intercourse will cease between us.**

A If sex is so trivial to her that she can cheerfully give it up, perhaps you should look at the reasons why this could be so. Has she ever had an orgasm with you? Are you sure? Would she prefer a change of sexual routine? Is she saying sex without fertility is wrong? (Where does this belief come from? Is it Church teaching?) Is she serious about her abstinence, or perhaps expressing a coded anxiety? You need to consider all these factors before reviewing your options, which may include counselling, celibacy, masturbation or an affair.

Q **At 45 I am no longer eager to make love to my wife. She is panicking about the future of our entire relationship.**

A Well if she is, that is your starting point to offer reassurance. Explain why you think your sexual interest has waned. Demonstrate very clearly that love and sex are separable by cuddling, hugging and caressing her freely. If she finds the passing of frequent sex an event to mourn, display your patience not hostility. She needs to talk through her sadness and feel that you have listened to her. Obviously if sex has been her means of obtaining marital 'security', these alternative strategies on your part should achieve the same result. But if you actually want less of a relationship altogether, you should come clean rather than shift the blame onto sex.

Q **Since having a hysterectomy, my wife has become very anxious that I will no longer want to make love to her. Why is she so fearful?**

A How would you feel if surgeons removed your testicles? Jolly? Sexy? Optimistic? No, of course you wouldn't. You'd feel like your wife – worried about your sexual attractiveness and identity. You might even get depressed. You'd certainly need a lot of patient understanding from family and friends. Note: if your wife's ovaries were taken along with her womb, she might also need to consider starting hormone replacement therapy.

Q **My wife has become sexually apathetic in her late 40s, and going through the motions is a turn-off.**

A Then don't go through the motions but buy some massage oil or cream and caress her naked body (especially her genitals) so that she feels much more sensual about being in bed with *you*. It may be that, pre-menopausally, she is experiencing vaginal dryness which is making sex quite unpleasant for her. These artificial lubricants will help.

Q **My husband has virtually stopped approaching me for sex, though I'm still considered to be an attractive woman.**

A Then instead of just protesting, see if his behaviour isn't trying to send you a message. Possibly, he would like you to approach him? When was the last time you said *he* was an attractive man? Are there sexual anxieties sapping his confidence? For instance, is he concerned about losing his erection? It would make sense for you to offer him greater penile stimulation during foreplay when you do have sex, and to vary this with evenings of body caressing when intercourse is not attempted although orgasm for both of you remains on the menu. If this proves *not* to be the answer, then take your worries to a professional counsellor.

Q **Does sex drive cease in mid-life?**

A Put it this way. If suitable partners continue to be available and sexual encounters are mutually gratifying, desire persists well into old age.

Q **My husband is very restless and claims to be impotent but I know he is still masturbating. Is it me or is he lying?**

A If he *is* lying, for what reasons might he be avoiding sex with you? If he isn't, then you should know that it is possible to be selectively impotent (i.e. in one situation, with one person, but not with another, or by yourself). Either way, though, something will be the cause and your best tactic is to give him permission to say 'anything and everything'.

Theories you might consider aloud include 'Are you bored with me? Are you angry with me? Are you worried about performing? Is something missing from our sexual pattern? Have you any fantasies or fetishes I've overlooked? Would you like to share erotic photos and videos with me? Would you like to talk about my erotic fantasies? Are you having an affair? Do you feel I'm too much like your mother? Am I being punished for something someone else has done? Do you feel impotent in our relationship as a whole, and not just sexually? Talk to me!'

Q My wife who has always been easy-going has changed now she is in her 40s. She is so moody and snappy – how can I jolly her out of it?

A You probably cannot, although she'll be grateful if you remain loving despite her behaviour. Treat these mood swings as a temporary affliction brought on by family and personal mid-life changes. Perhaps the children are leaving home. Certainly, she is approaching the end of her child-bearing years. Whenever possible, suggest she talks about it but be aware she may bite your head off for your trouble. Don't 'reward' the tetchiness but do attempt to make 'seasonal adjustments' – 'My wife is not quite herself at present so I decline to take everything she says either literally or personally'. There's a good chance her basic personality will eventually re-emerge.

Q My husband is still gorgeous, while I have lost my looks. How can I cope with other women wanting him when no man looks at me?

A If your husband were showing you enough attention, it's unlikely you'd be asking this question, so focus as much on the relationship *between* you, as on that between you and the outside world. Why have you two drifted apart? And are you also occupied with personal projects that give you valuable feelings of self-worth? (If not, why not?)

Q **Do women in their 40s make suitable partners for younger men?**

A Biologically, yes. Women reach their maximum capacity to have orgasms and multiple orgasms in their late 30s and early 40s. They also feel generally more comfortable with their sexuality by this stage, far removed from virginal insecurity. Men, by contrast, are at their sexual peak from 18 to 22, able to have several orgasms a day with small intervening time-gaps. They often make vigorous, athletic lovers. The drawbacks to this arrangement are usually emotional – either one side or the other tends to possess an unhealthy concentration of power making the other feel over-vulnerable. That apart, age is no bar to *any* loving attachment.

Q **Why does a middle-aged man want to start all over again with an immature girl half his age when he is married to an attractive, sexually-adept woman?**

A Because this is his last chance to live a complete cycle of life with another person who may bring him some of the emotional compensations he craves. First, she is 'half his age', which helps him feel rejuvenated. He can even look forward to becoming a father again. Second, she's 'immature', so there is more opportunity to mould her to his values. Third, she is less 'sexually-adept', allowing him to feel more like a sexual maestro than he otherwise could. Fourth, she cannot see through him as 'a desperate, ageing male who ought to know better', which seems to be the basis of your current evaluation. Other explanations would focus on your husband's inability to deal with declining powers except by making new erotic conquests. Instead of reorganizing his inner feelings, this man could well be coping with anxiety by taking a sexual 'tranquillizer'. He wouldn't be the first.

Q **At 42 I'm bored by my husband's sexual routine. How can I change it?**

A You cannot change him directly, you can only change yourself, although this may well have the effect of challenging him into new ways too. Issue an advance warning of your intention and use his language. For instance, if he's in business, say you're going to 'do an audit on yourself' to improve *your* personal performance (this approach is tactically wiser than indicating he could be boring). If he's in marketing, say you feel the need for a product overhaul (you could conceivably make this funny).

Start with simple changes. Lie on the *other* side of the bed from that which you habitually occupy. Go to bed earlier than usual with an invitation for him to join you (even without mentioning sex). If you normally protect yourself with a heavy nightdress, wear nothing. If you normally wear nothing, get yourself a seductive nightgown. If he wears boring pyjamas, buy him a silken nightshirt. If he normally makes the first move, just start innocently caressing him instead. If he invariably offers routine foreplay (kisses, breast-squeeze, entry) play much harder to get, or initiate a complete quickie. If he never goes down on you, go down on him and sort of edge towards a 69. Whatever happens by routine, imagine and implement the *opposite*. Golden rule – don't do this every night. Routine has served you well down the years because it contains the essence of a viable compromise of satisfactory behaviours. Always stress that you are changing yourself because that's the need *you* feel. Who knows, before long he could be suggesting intriguing uses for green nettles (see next question).

Q **Are stinging nettles sexually dangerous? My husband says he's heard they can be quite exciting when applied to the private parts.**

A They are fun as well as safe but only for those who 'like' a morsel of pain along with their pleasure. Dried nettles are less perturbing than fresh. Applied to the genitals or fissure of the buttocks, they cause limited congestion of the blood vessels, heightening desire. The Romans enjoyed 'urticaria' (nettle-rash) as part of foreplay. Mildly painful stimulation, by the way, is erotic because all arousal travels along the same neural pathways. If you are aroused by violence, for instance, your threshold of sexual excitement goes up too. It is called 'stimulus transformation'.

Q **Her: Why are my orgasms getting weaker and harder to achieve when I still enjoy sex as much as ever?**

A You are probably having less frequent sex than before, which means the vaginal muscles are not as 'fit' as they could be. More intercourse or masturbation could improve the situation as can simple tense-and-relax exercises for the vagina. Age and the menopause play a part – you actually *need* more stimulation than before. Don't worry, enjoy it (also see question on page 65).

Q **Him: I think my ejaculations are failing in strength – could this be true?**

A Yes, but this diminution will neither destroy your pleasure nor undermine your virility. Semen is only expelled with vigour to facilitate impregnation, and even then the difference it makes is marginal.

Q On the nights we don't make love I masturbate. Is this an immature practice in middle age?

A A purity campaigner might say yes, regarding masturbation as a teenage vice to be discarded upon reaching years of marital discretion. Sex therapists, doctors and sensualists would say no, regarding masturbation as a delight in its own right possessing therapeutic and calming properties while also keeping sexuality active when by force of circumstance a partnership is unable to do this. (In a democracy, *you* decide).

Q How often should couples make love in middle age?

A How often should you tell someone you love them? ('Gather ye rosebuds while ye may . . .') For the record, surveys show that couples in their early 40s average twice a week and those in their late 40s three times a fortnight. Some will of course exceed and some fall below this figure.

Q My husband suffers from middle-aged spread. I still love his body but he is embarrassed. He won't undress in front of me and the lights in our bedroom always have to be out.

A Are we talking general indulgence or specific beer-gut? If the former, initiate a joint but gentle change of basic diet plus exercise. If the latter, tell him you are worried about his heart, blood pressure and rate of memory-loss from all that booze. Try to find out which problems he wants to hide by drowning them in calories and alcohol. At the same time, explain how you *can* feel attracted to someone with a portly profile. He is probably convinced you feel as ashamed of it as he does, when we know you don't.

Q **My husband says if I don't give him as much sex as he likes he will go elsewhere.**

A These seem like immature and demanding postures. If he's serious, we fear the worst. However, it is possible he has recently felt threatened by your declining interest in sex and so has done some threatening of his own in return. It's cards on the table time. Find out how he feels. Does he value the marriage? Is he worried you don't love him any more? Or is he only after frequent supplies of 'one thing' in which case you might want to tell him to count you out.

Q **I don't seem to want intercourse any more, although I can still have orgasms by myself.**

A Nothing unusual in that – it's perfectly possible to have orgasms with very little actual arousal. Desire and climax can be distinct. You have to ask yourself whether your problem could be caused by boredom, apprehension, anger, stress, depression, inhibition or some unconscious reaction to intimacy perhaps reaching back into difficult relationships from the past.

Q Six years ago I was a beautiful young man with thick curly hair. Now I'm going bald and I can't see any women fancying me.

A Women don't date hanks or heads of hair and there's no evidence to show they are deterred from going out with men who have normal male pattern baldness. You are feeling less confident for some *other* reason and projecting this fear onto the boring but unavoidable fact that, in common with about half the male population world-wide, you have shed some top hair during middle-life. The function of this process of projection is to *protect* you from having to risk asking women out, thereby ensuring that you stay unrejected but also single.

Perhaps your youthful good looks were actually a disadvantage since they made women fall into your arms? As a result, you didn't have to learn courtship skills. In this sense, you could even be a little backward or a 'late starter'. Possibly that is the anxious feeling you daren't examine? Or possibly your insecurity stems from deeper experience? Either way, the truth is clear. Your hair loss proves you to be a normal, virile male with the right levels of sex hormone in circulation (testosterone triggers baldness, following a genetic blueprint). Don't look at your head for an answer, look at your heart. In the history of your life, who has made you feel insignificant? Which memories can still make you feel like crying today? Try to release these and any feeling of trauma.

Q Do all men become impotent eventually?

A Only in extreme old age – the American sex researcher Alfred Kinsey, for example, found that 75 per cent of all males aged 80+ were impotent.

Q Can the doctor prescribe anything to improve my sex life? I am 48 and suffering from intermittent impotence.

A It's a broad question. Many men who suffer from impotence have perfectly normal levels of the main male sex hormone testosterone. (It's been known for men who have lost their testes to continue to function sexually.) However, some men with abnormally low levels of (available) sex hormone do benefit from three intramuscular injections of testosterone to jolt their natural production into better working order. Testosterone in tablet form, on the other hand, does not offer the same benefit, although there is often some placebo effect. Given orally it appears to encourage the body to rely on the artificial supply rather than boost normal secretions.

The other principal drug offering hope is papaverine hydrochloride. This is injected into the cavernous spaces of the penis almost immediately causing erection. It is also useful for diagnostic purposes. If the patient cannot erect, despite the injection, then there is clear evidence of some sort of physical damage. Moreover, those with quite serious physical complaints (multiple sclerosis, diabetes mellitus etc) find that this drug will often permit response where none was possible previously. Hypertensive patients benefit more from papaverine than from psychological therapy. Single men can also be helped for the first time, as can the man who loses his erection because of premature ejaculation, since the drug sustains lovemaking capacity beyond orgasm.

However, there are drawbacks to treatments with papaverine, not least of which is priapism (non-stop erection) which after 12 hours would become a medical emergency. The injections are in themselves unaesthetic and really require medical supervision. Papaverine should not be used to boost the stud abilities of normally functioning men, or when going on holiday, or when starting a new relationship. The treatment cannot substitute for counselling where impotence is produced by a poor quality of relationship. (Drugs cannot do your talking for you.) The techniques of behavioural therapy in getting couples to pay greater attention to sex education, the importance of touch and the need for good communication cannot be replaced. Otherwise, the drug is safe insofar as anyone can tell. More than 10,000 patients suffering from varieties of impotence have now been treated in the USA with vasoactive drugs related to papaverine.

Q **I hate the idea of injecting my body with chemicals because I'm sure there will always be unwelcome side effects. Can my doctor help me overcome premature ejaculation and loss of erection in any other way?**

A Yes, he or she can refer you for all sorts of therapy from implant surgery to the use of an ingenious but harmless device called the 'Correctaid'. This is basically a condom of soft transparent silicone rubber with an incorporated tube. The penis is introduced into the open end. The tube is sucked to produce a vacuum which gently draws the penis into the sheath and causes it to expand and fill the device. With the erect penis filling the Correctaid, the tube is closed, then wrapped closely around the base of the penile shaft. 'Wearing the Correctaid like a condom with the vacuum intact keeps the penis erect for as long as desired', say the manufacturers. Perhaps 45 per cent of men ejaculate within two minutes of penetration but with this device, sex can continue even after you have had your (first) climax. The device comes in several sizes and reportedly lasts for two to three years.

Q Although I am unfulfilled, I decided against an affair because I think it is wrong. Instead, I took up studying. My husband has reacted to this as jealously as if I *were* having an affair.

A Which only goes to show that the mechanics of jealousy don't depend upon a sexual scenario. It sounds as though your husband resents you spending time on anything that doesn't concern him. He feels left out, neglected, excluded, rejected, plotted against. You yourself would admit to inadequacies in the marriage. But the problem is to decide whether the jealousy is *only* to do with his long-standing paranoia or whether it's partly related to your refusal to face up to the issues dividing you. People can feel madly jealous (and jealously mad) if you give them a mixed message: 'I love you, don't touch me', or 'You are my life partner, you can *never* make me happy'.

Q My husband has had an affair and I feel destroyed. I'm not sure I will ever be able to let him near me again.

A Notice that you are not saying the marriage has ended. Instead you are registering the 'appropriate' feelings of someone let down in an ongoing relationship. You are shocked. You are angry. You appear to feel as if you had been 'bombed'. You can only see, at present, that sexual intercourse with this 'enemy' is unthinkable. And at present it certainly is. Sex might become possible in the future if you can go through the reasons for the affair, if you can tell him exactly how it has made you feel, if he can show you he understands every jot of your reaction, while still putting in a plea on behalf of his own fallibility. No, you won't want to take him to bed today. But that is not the pressing issue – sex is the language in which you are expressing your loss of trust.

Q I'm having an affair and paradoxically this has improved sex with my husband.

A They say the more you have the more you want, and not just money. It is physically true of sex. Your illicit liaison provides excitement, eroticism and increased physical arousal some of which is being directed towards your husband. However, fear and guilt can also be arousing. Perhaps you're trying to take extra care to keep him sweet at home?

Q I'm happy to have intercourse even when I don't feel sexy because I usually climax anyway. Why therefore won't my husband let me stimulate him when desires are reversed, i.e. when I want it but he does not?

A The simple answer is because he is different. What's right for you doesn't suit him and possesses a different psychological meaning. Perhaps he's anxious; perhaps he's 'fastidious'; perhaps he's selfish. We suspect the real gripe is that you aren't always able to have sex when you want and that you end up feeling thwarted. You can only attempt to negotiate for more of what you like.

Q Can illness lower your sex drive?

A In general, any lowering, depressing or enervating condition is a turn off. Try to feel sexy next time you have flu. Sufferers from angina, arthritis, asthma, circulation disorders, renal disease, sclerosis, myalgic encephalomyelitis, strokes and spinal injuries can have specific libido problems.

Q **Is it normal to lose sexual interest after surgery?**

A Very much so, because the body is always 'traumatized' by it. Surgery and anaesthesia can also cause depressive episodes which in turn destroy sexual desire. The following operations will most affect sexual interest and performance: episiotomy, hysterectomy, ileostomy, colostomy, ileal conduit, mastectomy, rectal surgery, vaginal repair, prostatectomy, lumbar sympathectomy, spinal surgery, and any section work on ovaries, penis or testicles. Even routine prostate procedures may damage the veinous network supplying blood to the genitals.

Q **My husband used a vibrator to give me orgasms. Could this prevent me from climaxing normally?**

A There is no truth in the suggestion that women get addicted to battery-operated plastic dildos. This was a male worry about becoming superfluous current in the 1970s which events have not confirmed. Instead of limiting sexual opportunities, vibrators have expanded them so that the principal consequence of their use is increased ease of climax under *a wide variety* of conditions.

Q My husband wants me to wear stockings and suspenders in bed, but at my age I feel such a fool.

A Then tell him if he wants to get his way he will have to make you feel comfortable in your role. That means masses of reassurance and loving kindness. Only then will you notice that nobody else is in the bedroom, nobody else will know what is happening, and perhaps it is a small favour that he has asked. Of course, there's nothing to stop you requesting an erotic treat in return . . . Remember, your clothes aren't what he loves *instead* of you – they are only a means to the end of being able to show his love *for* you.

Q I've heard that yogis can control their erections to last forever. Is this true?

A What's called 'operant conditioning' may be used by expert meditators to control pulse, brain waves and sexual response. However, just as most ordinary mortals cannot bring themselves to walk on live coals, lie on beds of nails or stop their heartbeats altogether, so they find it practically impossible to 'will an erection'.

Q I found a contact magazine in my husband's briefcase with adverts for 'threesomes' ringed in pencil. Does this mean he's being unfaithful?

A It must mean he's having thoughts or fantasies along those lines. You've obviously questioned his trustworthiness or you wouldn't have sleuthed in his bag. If you want to repair the marital damage, we suggest you take your entire relationship out for examination, rather than introduce this awkwardly-obtained evidence. Just say that you feel very cut off from him – does he feel as detached from you?

Q **I began a relationship with a new girlfriend last month. The sex is fantastic, but I'm a little surprised by how frequently she slips her thumb into my anus whenever we get started.**

A All we can say is that she intends to please and that often lovers will do to you what they would like you to do to them.

Q **I am beginning to recover from impotence thanks to the help of a wonderful therapist. My erections do not last long enough to satisfy my partner, but I am bursting with sexual desire.**

A You can obviously talk this over with the person trying to treat your condition, but it is a paramount rule of sex therapy that new frustrations should not be added to the old. Although you were probably advised to abstain from intercourse as part of the help programme this does not mean you should never have climaxes, either by yourself or from your partner's hands on 'non therapy' days. You don't even need an erection to enjoy ejaculation. Ask your partner to apply the head of a vibrator to the upper surface of your penis just below the coronal ridge, switch it on, and you'll see what we mean.

Q My new husband and I are very much in love. How can we furnish the bedroom for maximum pleasure?

A This is usually a question asked by a starry-eyed young couple lacking in experience, so we guess that is how you must be feeling. You need a firm mattress on a bed-frame that doesn't rock or squeak. You need a double bed large enough for both to sleep almost singly on restless nights. You need to warm your bed in a warm room. You need orthopaedically-correct pillows to support your head. (As many necks get ricked during sex as when driving.) You need a fleece on the floor for lovemaking that falls out of bed. You need ceiling mirrors *only* if the idea pleases you. You need a lock on the door, plus double-glazing and sound proofing if you can afford it. Music is a bonus, massage oil is a must and televisions and telephones should be banned. Then you just need one another.

7　Special sexualities

Q **I am irresistibly drawn towards things considered to be rude or even 'kinky'. Is this so unnatural?**

A A famous English sexologist said 'Most people have at least one preferred sex behaviour which a judge would find odd'. To which you could add: 'Just as most judges probably have at least one preferred sex behaviour which most juries would find odd'. This is so because we all possess what are called 'pre-genital needs'. Long before puberty attempts to fix our adult sexual direction (often unsuccessfully), we've appeared in the long running drama of being a child. As infants, we either played the lead or the walk-on, were well or badly treated in a comedy or a tragedy. Whatever the denouement, we learned certain lessons from our roles, above all about what we wanted *more* of. We've all met characters who are touch hungry, or seriously shy or armour-plated, just as we come to realize that some people primarily gratify those needs during sexual contact with us. For example, 'the woman who loves too much' (see Robin Norwood's best-selling book of the same title) 'enjoying' her masochistic roles; or the infantile man craving his dummy and nappies.

To change the metaphor, when puberty does come along, some of these attitudes are re-sexualized like a developing photograph placed in a bath of 'fixer'. At the same time, many other objects or actions snapped by the camera get trapped in the sexual picture. So if a shy young man discovering masturbation plays with his sister's underwear, the very pleasure he takes will establish the connection in his brain between panties and sex. He may go on to have a fetish, get more interested in cross-dressing or learn, like you, that sex is a fertile garden in which almost any plant will grow. In summary, your 'kinky' interest can be variously interpreted as fear of sex, joy in sex, insecurity or curiosity, damage or dynamism, main personality or accidental attribute.

Q **My boyfriend is a well-known popstar. It's difficult enough to have an ordinary relationship because of his career but we were doing well until he told me his secret longing. He wants me to mother him constantly. I'm supposed to dress him in a nappy and change him when he's wet. I don't really mind but I am confused.**

A If you don't mind, you don't mind; but we guess you are asking whether he's able to offer you a loving future despite his foible. Given his fetish, it would be likely for him to err towards self-centredness. Ask yourself if he's deserved your generosity? Draw some very clear boundaries around any 'games' he wants to play. Tell him it's not going to be one-sided. You may not have a comparable need of your own, but we're sure you can think of a way to say 'Tonight we are going to do exactly what *I* want'. The problem with some infantile fantasies is that gratification may lead to growing up – and out of the relationship which served them.

Q **Is there any way to tell if you're bisexual?**

A Well, we're not born with a serial number tattooed on our foreheads. This question is often asked by people having bad heterosexual experiences who feel sexually frustrated. It is also put by those who find themselves institutionally trapped in a one-sex environment – private school, prison, armed forces, religious order, polar expedition or exclusive club. Freud suggested everyone has bisexual potential because we are born with the capacity to enjoy 'polymorphous pleasure'. This may well be true, but we're also conditioned from birth to channel our experience in one direction or another – and occasionally in both. Genuine behavioural bisexuality seems confined to those who, while bonding normally with a mate of one sex, still crave ongoing physical and emotional contact with the alternative sex. We can all love people regardless of gender but most of us don't wish to express physical bisexuality unless deprived of other possibilities.

Q **I have read of auto-fellation. Is this possible?**

A Yes, but it is an extremely exhausting means of acquiring a stiff neck. Usually confined to the ultra-curious young.

Q **Should I tell my boyfriend about my fantasy to paint his face and dress him in my petticoat? It turns me on every time I think of it.**

A What is his likely reaction? Is he rigid or flexible in his sexual thinking? Does he always stick to masculine conventions or is there a comfortable 'feminine' side to his personality? Some men would run a mile; some would say great. (Some men would even run away *because* it's a secretly attractive idea.) See if he likes being stroked with your satiny petticoat to start with.

Q **After too much to drink, I woke up the other night to find my boyfriend having sex with me. I can only say he was shivering with ecstasy and muttering that this was his greatest wish come true. Is this possible?**

A Yes, it even has a name – hypnophilia – he's a 'sleep lover'. He revels in the masterful sense of possession provided by your unconscious form. His fantasy will have a history and it would be prudent to check it out – is there more to come?

Q **What should you do when you get an obscene phone call? I'm still shaking.**

A Break the contact as soon as you realize what is happening. Tell the police and the phone company if there's a repeat. Talk to a friend about your distress. Do not play games with any nuisance caller because their game is getting you to play. About 99.7 per cent of these calls are made by frightened, harmless men. There is no erotic power in their inner lives so they compensate at your expense. But you must beware the 0.3 per cent who play for keeps.

Q **When I picked up the extension, I overheard my husband dialling one of those phone-sex services. I never deny him sex. Why would he do this?**

A Probably out of curiosity rather than sexual starvation. For a change he wanted to hear a woman accept all his sexual tendencies, however deviant, albeit for money, by using her imagination. You can choose whether to ignore it, condemn it or learn from it. We only suggest you ensure *he* pays the phone bill.

Q **When my fiancé rang me the other night he started getting fresh on the phone, asking me to tell him what I was wearing under my dress. Then he seemed to get very out of breath.**

A Separated lovers have abused the telephone for decades. You must have realized what he meant when he said he *couldn't* wait to see you again?

Q **Why is it men who are perverted?**

A Because men are biologically more aggressive and socially more privileged than women, seizing the leading pathological roles in life as well. One feminist defined a man as 'testosterone poisoning on two legs'. Some biological thinkers believe men have 'overlap' sexuality. They are so easily aroused they seek gratification far beyond the original 'stimulus target'. (It was Adam in the Garden of Eden who was rumoured to have copulated with every beast of the field.)

Q **My new girlfriend wears several big hoop earrings. She tells me she loves the feel of metal through her flesh. No problem. But can I believe her when she says she has other more intimate piercings on her body? We haven't yet made love.**

A From what she has said, why not? The 'erotic' infibulation of nipples and labia is a well-known phenomenon in many cultures. It is also one of the few sexual 'paraphilias' (or deviations) attracting a female following. Is it something you really don't want to deal with? Then don't.

Q **My brother-in-law is a 'kisser' and he doesn't stop at women. It's how he greets the *men* in his family, and as a conservative male I can't stand it.**

A Then try to convert the kiss into a hug and if this does not work have a little chat. You are up against a cultural barrier here but remember embracing a man does not define you sexually. You might just as well ask if the President of France is gay since he kisses his ministers in the morning.

Q I believe in women's rights but when making love to my husband my favourite fantasy is to imagine a dirty old tramp forcing me to fellate him.

A Which only goes to show that we cannot choose our fantasies any more than we can select our dreams. Fantasies appeal because they generate personal sexual energy. Morally, you are striving for a better world of feminine equality but that pressure almost traps you into finding pictures of your 'worst fears' erotically disturbing. On the other hand, there may be an abrasing wish in your soul actually to be mistreated by a man, yet you could still argue this was only because you got accustomed to male abuse when young (perhaps literally), so the idea is only 'attractive' on grounds of familiarity.

Q **I am a closet cross-dresser. Should I tell my wife?**

A It is probably your greatest wish to have a partner who understands that transvestites are mainly heterosexual men happy with their gender who either have a fetish for female clothing or from time to time wish their appearance to be interpreted as female; that they are motivated by a powerful compulsion arising from childhood associations; and that they either inject sexuality into the desired clothing, becoming adrenalized with excitement by wearing it, or they can only achieve relaxed tranquillity by shedding the masculine burden along with male attire.

Partners respond variously. Some acquire a 'sister' to put beside the husband they already know. Some reject the effeminate component they discover included in their husband's identity. To answer *your* question, you need to decide whether the compulsion is getting unavoidably stronger, whether your wife seems to be in any way receptive to conversation on the subject, and what you have to lose if things go wrong. Family courts contain few sexual radicals when it comes to the custody of children, for instance. There is probably a transvestite helpline in your area. Contact them before making any irrevocable move.

Q **Something funny is happening in our street. Whenever I hang out my washing, certain items disappear, usually underwear. Should I tell the police?**

A Yes, they'll understand there's a 'kleptolagniac' in the neighbourhood (a man, sometimes a youth, who gets erotic pleasure from stealing favoured items of clothing, usually for the purposes of masturbation). Since he seems so persistently interested in your wardrobe, the police might even ask you to set a special trap.

Q I am a fireman in a small town. I have *always* wanted to change my sex. What will happen to my wife and children?

A When you make your announcement they will simultaneously be relieved and confused. First, lots of your past behaviour will suddenly make sense. But second, they are going to have to adjust their identities as the relatives of someone they thought was a man who now appears to be a woman. Shock can make people sad or angry, depressed or rejecting. There will obviously be comment in your local community which will affect them too. But if you are determined to go ahead, you must be clear that the outcome *is* unpredictable. Some male-to-female transsexuals lose touch with their families altogether – others remain as companions to their wives. Some small towns make merciless fun – others are completely unfazed. Some employers discriminate – others only care about your ability in the job. Break the news gently and emphasize that you are still the same person from the inside looking out.

Q As I get older, I become more anxious when reading about sex attacks on women pensioners. I cannot believe anyone could be so cruel, nor can I see why they do it.

A As most people now realize, rape is primarily a crime of violence taking a sexual form. The principal motive is either to hurt and humiliate the woman or to act out the perpetrator's view that women are sub-human. Since women cannot rape men, the crime has always been regarded by society as a cowardly attack by the stronger on the weaker sex. This makes it all the more likely that very old women *will* be included in the ambit of attack, since they are numerous (women outlive men by about a decade) and they often live in circumstances of supreme vulnerability. However, there are also men called 'gerontophiles' who experience specific sexual attraction towards the old, and this group accounts for a small proportion of the attacks mentioned in the press.

Q While standing in a crowded train, I felt what I took to be an umbrella handle pressing into my buttocks. I said nothing, but when we got to the station I saw the man next to me had no umbrella and nothing in his hands. Was it what I think it was?

A We're afraid so. You encountered a 'frotteur', one who presses himself sexually against people in a public place, another instance of male sexual harassment. The attraction seems to be the difficulty of proving the offence coupled with its ease of deniability.

Q I am new to London but already in four weeks I've been flashed at six times in the subway. Tell me it's not my fault.

A It's not your fault. Ask any woman living in a large city and she will confirm a similar experience. Nothing is really done about the problem because men rarely expose themselves to other men, so the issue doesn't register with the male authorities. You may think it best to ignore the exposer but there's nothing wrong with playing this joke in your mind at the same time. Flasher (revealing his equipment): 'What do you think of that then, girlie?' His victim: 'Oh, I thought it was like a penis, only smaller'.

Q I can't believe what I've heard – that some people actually drink their own urine!

A The late Indian Prime Minister Mr Desai had a glass of his own every morning. A movement called 'The Auto-Bionomists' consume their own urine with the fervour of a health fad. Sexually, many prostitutes offer 'golden showers' to clients seeking 'humiliation'. Some of the urine is drunk. The great sexologist, Henry Havelock Ellis was, in private, a urine-fetishist or 'urolagniac'. It is in fact almost inevitable that a process so biologically bound up with sexuality (just think of the male urethra) should become sexualized. In favour of Desai and Co, you can at least say that fresh urine is clean and sterile.

Q **Why are young girls these days afflicted with nymphomania? Is it something in the food or the water?**

A Neither, and they are not, and nor is our age more sinful than the last. In the middle of the reign of Queen Victoria, there were 80,000 female prostitutes on the streets of London alone, sex with children of 12 was legal and there were no statutes prohibiting incest. In 19th century rural Scotland, girls freely had affairs and the mother of one pregnant unmarried daughter reflected, 'It was not so bad as if she had stolen twopence that was not her own'. We have already commented on the widespread use of the term nymphomaniac as a mistaken synonym for 'a woman who is sexually active'. True nymphomania is a rare type of schizoid psychosis, dementia or manic depression (whichever classification you prefer) often associated with damage to that area of the brain known as the amygdala, or with severe hormonal imbalance and most such mental patients are readily perceived to be 'crazed'.

Q **Is there a male equivalent to nymphomania?**

A Yes, it's called 'satyriasis' and is characterized by indiscriminate attempts at coupling or compulsive masturbation. Not to be confused with 'priapism' which simply means a state of persistent erection often produced in the absence of sexual desire. Unrelieved priapism is a potential health emergency.

Q **My boyfriend wants to spank me.**

A Playful slaps and cuffs are a feature of foreplay for many mammals, including humans. Spanking the bottom draws blood into the lower abdomen thus promoting arousal. However, some people are dedicated disciplinarians, preferring slaps to any alternative sex preliminary and you must decide for yourself how far (if at all) you wish to go.

Q **My boyfriend wants me to cane him.**

A Unless it's a whim, this means he seriously enjoys sexual discipline and probably has little capacity to enjoy other arousal patterns. Unless you share his interest, you could get seriously bored. He probably wants to act out specific domination fantasies with you. Are you interested?

Q **My boyfriend wants me to be his sex slave.**

A Now you have to decide whether you really wish to enter the world of 'sado-masochistic' or 'SM' sex. Don't confuse this with cruel mutilation and sex killing. You are being asked to engage in roleplay, the entire point of which is to explore the fine line between domination and submission with the receiver remaining in charge. Read Pauline Reage's *Histoire d'O* for one celebrated (if over-the-top) version of this fantasy.

Q **Why would anyone want to bring pain into their love lives? It seems crazy!**

A Because pain and pleasure use the same nerve circuits in the body so if you heighten one you heighten the other. However, there is a clear limit between what you might call the 'pleasure of pain' and its unpleasantness. Being tapped on the rump might be titillating, being flogged might be excruciating. For some people, however, their pain-tolerance is extraordinarily, even preternaturally high. This may partly be due to 'practice'. But it may also be due to their strong secondary motivation to gain pleasure from punishment. Among the motives might be acute sexual guilt (which being whipped might appease); an irresistible desire to swap power-roles (the mighty judge in real life becoming the humiliated drudge in foreplay with a dominatrix); and acute sexual nostalgia (school corporal punishment during puberty having firmly imprinted a connection between apprehension, caning and arousal). If you finally analyse this behaviour you come down to 'the generation of excitement through sexual drama'.

Q **Why would anyone want to be flogged until they bleed?**

A Because they have intense feelings of self-loathing or powerful desires for 'purification'. Self-flagellation was common in religious orders down the centuries. The injunction to 'mortify' the flesh is based on the peculiar dualism in Christian and other doctrines regarding the body as a sinful entity divorced from the healthy mind. The great Victorian Prime Minister Gladstone was a powerful instance. He spent five nights out of seven wandering the streets of London accosting prostitutes in an attempt to get them to mend their ways. Then he'd go home and beat himself bloody because the exercise had obviously challenged his physical resistance to their blandishments.

Q **My girlfriend wants me to 'humiliate' her before we make love. I don't know what she means.**

A Then you should probably say that her request is outside your experience and if you wish to get involved ask for some guidelines. We guess your partner is either someone quite professionally high-powered, or has suggestive memories of childhood teasing and abasement.

Q **Is it true that all women are masochists at heart?**

A No. The social reality is that women are vulnerably underprivileged in relation to men. This being so, they have often been forced to appease their lords and masters, but there's no need to turn this into a sexual grand theory. Do prisoners worship their chains?

Q My husband wants me to wear a G-string and see-through negligee in bed.

A On all surveys, most men seem to feel the same way. Something in male personality makes them respond sexually to any object or item of clothing encountered during sex-play or brought into the 'mating-room'. Visual arousal is obviously most stimulated by garments half-revealing your physical charms, or those fitted next to your genitals.

Q My husband wants me to wear a 'waspie' waist cincher, directoire knickers, fishnet stockings, black high-heeled shoes, a leather belt and a black face-mask before we make love.

A Then he has a very 'programmed' set of sexual arousal cues, being on the borderline of fetish-dependency. As ever, you must decide whether the candle's worth the game!

Q My husband (a doctor) insists I wear wellington boots in bed otherwise he claims he can't make love to me. He's basically mean with money but I can spend any amount I like in a rainwear store.

A A wholly dependent fetishist like your husband can no longer 'look sex in the eye'. His functioning is confined to erotic reflections or associations, in this case sexualized rubber footwear, as if the 'real' thing were a Gorgon with the power to destroy him. The boots may also work as a 'substitute skin' – rubber does possess tactile qualities rather like the human original – while at the same time remaining impervious, non-porous, protective, even prophylactic. They say it's tough to be in love with a thing. It's even tougher to be in love with a thing-lover. He sounds both demanding and controlling. Are you sure this is your partner for life? He could possibly be made more friendly by psychotherapy.

Q I love anal sex. Is that unusual for a woman?

A No. Your body is as well provided with nerve-endings in this region as that of men (although prostate gland sensation is denied to you) so the potential for physical pleasure is undeniable.

Q I've just found out my new girlfriend works
as a stripper. I begged her to give it up but she
says she's hooked on it. I don't understand.

A Perhaps she wasn't a very attractive teenager.
Now, as a hungrily-ogled woman, she is enjoying
her sexual power to the full. This exhibitionistic
streak is highly compensating, hence the wish to
continue with it. Your best bet is to let her find
out for herself for how long the ploy is viable and
you could help most by valuing all of her, not just
her boobs and bum. Life has probably taught her
that people *are* what they look like. You could
begin to alter that.

Q My husband tells me I've got to make love to
another man while he watches from the
closet.

A Well, you don't have to and this voyeuristic
ultimatum could be interpreted as simply unkind.
The overtones suggest your husband may have a
masochistic or even homosexual component
(wanting to feel humiliated; getting sexually close
to another man at one remove). Clearly he has
come to regard you as more like a possession than
a person. Perhaps you begin to see your
relationship this way as well?

Q The other night my girlfriend and I and two other friends all fell into bed after a party and quite a lot of sex took place. We did at least manage to use condoms.

A Well, we're thankful for that. Obviously, breaking taboos is always erotically exciting but are your friendships able to cope with this deepening physical contact? Even in the heady days of the 60s, 'swapping' always required stable characters with strong nerves, though it didn't always get them.

Q My boyfriend wants to give me an enema. Yuk!

A It takes all sorts. Colonic lavage, as it's called, is very popular in Germany but enema fetishism proper is usually restricted to those who first had them administered by nurses at school with predictably arousing consequences. Clearly you were not among their number.

Q My girlfriend wants me to tie her up. Yuk!

A Put simply, she is asking whether you will increase her capacity to respond to you sexually by reducing her power to control the predictability and timing of climax. You seem to be saying you won't and the two of you are headed for an impasse. Is your feeling really one of revulsion, or did you just get a shock?

Q I've found hundreds of photos of disabled people and cripples on crutches in my late uncle's bedroom, along with magazines like *Ampix*.

A Which means your late uncle was likely to have been an 'amputee fetishist', one who felt sexually excited by the disabled. Why? Precisely because the existence of disability in the 'love object' may have reduced an overall sense of anxiety about sexuality. Maybe this discovery is very disturbing, raising questions about your uncle's character, or filling your mind with unwanted personal associations. Just remember, there are more sides to people than you can see on the surface.

Q I'm a woman of 26 and feel really peculiar because I can only reach orgasm in a crouching or kneeling position.

A Some women can only masturbate by holding a pillow between their thighs and squeezing rhythmically. It is almost a matter of chance that certain sex positions provide the angle and degree of stimulation essential to your release while others do not. However, bear in mind that this may change should you take a differently-proportioned future partner, or learn to · experiment with a powerful vibrator.

Q My homosexual lover wants to give me electric shocks.

A He doesn't have to get what he wants. Faradic electricity has often been employed for a sexual purpose but you'd be a fool to rely on anyone's judgement about voltage other than your own.

Q I'm 15 and want to be a prostitute.

A We'd all like to make easy money but hooking is harder than it looks. Apart from obvious financial incentives, does the lifestyle have something personally appealing to you? Are you old and bitter before your time? Are you covering up for ill treatment previously received? Selling sex won't salve psychic wounds and money can only buy objects.

Q I was abused by my father from the age of 3 to the age of 14. I am devastated to find myself repeating the story with a neighbour's child.

A There is a connection between the two events – those who are abused often go on to abuse others – but explanation cannot be turned into absolution. Contact a counselling agency without delay.

Q My boyfriend says he accidentally set fire to our bed. He isn't a smoker yet he always carries a lighter, clicking it on and staring at the flame.

A The two likeliest explanations are hard drugs or 'pyrolagnia'. He's either shooting up and getting careless or he's erotically obsessed with burning things. We suggest you take extreme care.

Q **I possess a pet alsation and feel very peculiar when it gets a huge red erection.**

A When animals look sexually potent it can obviously disturb humans in two ways. First, they may also become aroused. Second, they may then regard the implications as perverse. You are not the first person to feel similarly uncomfortable. In fact, if any large red sex organ is waved in your face it's impossible not to think about – well, sex! This is quite different from wanting to take any further action.

Q **Am I perverted? I prefer my girlfriend to wash only every *other* day.**

A It was Napoleon who wrote to Josephine from the battlefield: 'Home in three days – don't wash'. You clearly share his preference for powerful sexual odour mixed with sweat (pheromones plus apocrine) which is a basic biological stimulant. Few humans did much body-cleansing prior to the nineteenth century which may explain why in our very sanitized modern world sexual desire came to be identified as a problem. If you're both happy . . .

Q **My lover gave me a terrible (but exciting) shock by putting an ice cube into my bottom. Is this dangerous?**

A The water isn't but people can and do die of shock. Sharp shards of ice can also pose an obvious hazard. You take your own risks.

Q **After I finished breast-feeding one night, my husband asked if he could be suckled as well.**

A He might just have been curious or jealous or he could be developing a fetish. Is he 'infantile' in other sexual ways? If you feel disturbed, let him know and find out more.

Q **My wife bought me a 'cock ring' as a jokey private Christmas present. Is there any point in trying it on?**

A Yes, if only to express a little gratitude and not be a stick-in-the-mud. It may not light your fuse, but a gentle constriction at the base of the penis has been claimed to augment both erectility and ejaculatory sensitivity.

Q **I had oral sex with my husband last night and I swear he tasted of asparagus.**

A This is because he had eaten asparagus during the preceding 24 hours and the aroma would be detectable in all his urethral secretions, particularly in his urine.

Q **Why do I get turned on by seeing bald-headed women?**

A Because hairlessness equals nakedness which suggests sexiness. Moreover, there is a similarity in the images of a circumcised penis and a bald head, again leading to sexual associations. You are also charged up by the unexpectedness of what you saw and alertness *is* arousal.

Q **My boyfriend asked me for a lock of my pubic hair. Is that a normal request?**

A Not statistically, since most men don't ask this of their lovers, but he may just have a lovely innocent feeling for your body. On the other hand, some notoriously disturbed individuals have formed similar collections and the very fact that you are asking us means you should get to know him better before becoming more deeply involved.

8   Sex grown old and wise?

Q   **What's the oldest age at which men and women may become parents?**

A   The US record for motherhood is held by Mrs Ruth Kistler who at the age of 57 years, 129 days gave birth to a daughter. The UK record goes to Mrs Winifred Wilson who had her tenth child when aged between 54 and 55 (her birthdate is uncertain). These achievements, however, may be superseded when new implantation techniques permit doctors to put fertilized eggs into women of any age, even those who are post-menopausal. The *Guinness Book Of Records* is remarkably sexist in not recording the age of the oldest father (or claimed father). Theoretically, men may sire offspring throughout life – Picasso was a notable example, begetting his last child when he was well into his 80s. We don't know why you have asked the question but in case you have the feeling that sex after 57 years and 129 days is inappropriate for a woman because natural conception won't occur, just imagine what you would have done with *all* your forty children had acts of sexual intercourse during your fertile years every ten months led to pregnancy. And why do men enjoy seven decades of fertility – because God wants them to take younger women as concubines? Surely that's male propaganda.

Q I find at the age of 60 that I can't have sexual intercourse as much as I'd like. This is a special problem because last year I married a woman ten years younger than me who obviously expects a fully active sexual relationship.

A Which she can have so long as she doesn't expect you to behave like a teenager with the reflexes of a leopard and the stamina of a stallion. You can take her to bed morning noon and night, for hand, mouth and cuddling bliss, but as Alex Comfort says:

'Age induces some irrevocable changes in human sexual performance. These are chiefly in the male for whom orgasm becomes less frequent. It occurs in every second act of intercourse, or in one act in three, rather than every time. More direct physical stimulation too is needed to produce an erection. However, compared with, say, running ability, these changes are functionally minimal and actually tend in the direction more miles per gallon and greater, if less acute, satisfaction for both partners. In the absence of two disabilities – actual disease and the belief that the old are or should be asexual – sexual requirement and capacity are lifelong' (A Good Age, 1977).

Comfort expressed a similar idea more pithily in 1972: 'What stops you from having sex is the same thing that stops you from riding a bicycle – except it's later for sex.'

Q **My GP is surprised I still want sex in my 60s.**

A Training as a doctor does not insulate you from age-prejudice. Medical personnel also see so much physical disability that they tend to undervalue emotional or sexual losses. Fortunately, the general climate is changing. One recent advertiser in a magazine column was at pains to announce 'Woman, 67, *still sexually active*, seeks . . '. Much psychological insecurity lies behind age-prejudice. It has always been difficult for children to imagine their parents in coital clinches. To imagine their grandparents in similar embraces means not only challenging their incest fantasies but also confronting the power of sex without the protective canopy of a youthful skin. Yet the survey evidence is that seven out of ten couples over the age of 60 remain sexually active.

Q **I am on HRT hormone pills which keep me young and attractive with a very sensual skin, but I resent having to take them. I feel my husband only loves me for my looks and would stop if the pills ran out.**

A Well, that is a terrible feeling and needs to be separated from the medical pros and cons of taking HRT. Obviously you need to put pressure on your man to become a better companion and friend, rather than denying yourself what appear to be physical benefits. For what it's worth, we have come across this problem before. The woman we saw had *always* felt undervalued as a child, only winning some grudging admiration when during puberty she developed a big bust and generally earthy looks (although cousins continued to tease her mercilessly). Are there similar emotional skeletons in your past?

Q We were a swinging couple when younger and enjoyed 'partouzes' (sex parties), but now we've stopped on grounds of age and AIDS. As a result, my husband has gone into a decline and scarcely performs.

A Retirement is always painful, even from socially unconventional practices. Moving on means giving something up, so let him experience his term of mourning. You have both got to learn to adapt to a sexual lifestyle which will lack the familiar 'on button' (or 'safety valve') previously provided by group sex. It is extremely difficult to abandon established sexual patterns so, if it would help, why not enjoy films, videos, tapes, fantasies, descriptions or memories of the real thing as lawfully available?

Q I am terrified of losing my sex drive because I am getting older. I can already feel myself slowing down. Does HRT make a woman feel sexier?

A Straightforward HRT offers you synthetic oestrogen and progesterone. These may do wonders for your skin, bones and overall well-being, but won't necessarily increase your levels of desire. Ironically, the chemical in charge of libido in both sexes is the male hormone testosterone. Wise HRT specialists therefore include a little testosterone in their prescription, commonly in the form of a small implant. Talk to your specialist about this – but report at once any *unwanted* masculinizing effects should the dosage be too high (they are reversible).

Q Two years ago at the age of 65 I married for the first time. My 70-year-old husband enjoys sex a great deal but I find it very uncomfortable. How can things be improved?

A We guess you are suffering from vaginal soreness due to oestrogen deficiency. See your doctor about getting a local hormone cream which you can apply yourself. If the real problem is a failure on your new husband's part to pay attention to your sexual needs, vocalize your discontent. It might be an idea to 'do the sexological exam'. This consists of sitting together naked and taking it in turns to offer a stroke or caress anywhere on your partner's body. Then you both rate the touches on a scale of 'plus three to minus three' first for sensuality, then for sexuality. If you do this for an hour or so you will acquire body maps of each other's favourite erogenous zones and favoured styles of stimulation. It is an acceptable means of expressing preference and there's bound to be the odd surprise. For instance, one woman was astonished to find she liked the sides of her breasts stroked even more than the nipples. Equally amazed was her lover.

Q My husband is in his early 60s and has become overly concerned about his appearance. He spends hours in the bathroom applying hair restorer and 'anti-grey' gel. He keeps himself very fit. If asked, he lies about his age by up to 11 years. Our own sex life is fine but infrequent. Could this mean he is having an affair?

A It certainly means he would rather be graceful than grow old but whether for the delight of others or out of pure narcissism we don't know. You are really asking whether vanity or infidelity is more common. Reduced frequency of desire is not abnormal at his age. Why not ask for more cuddles at night and more joint outings by day? If he's all dressed up there should be somewhere to go.

Q My sex drive remains hearty but my husband doesn't respond. All he can suggest is that I masturbate. He's very set in his ways.

A You need to get tough with him and tell him a few home truths. Conjugal relations are the legitimate prerogative of any spouse. While you cannot force him to have sexual intercourse, you can make it clear that you do expect him to accompany you to bed for reasons other than sleep. There's nothing to stop him from holding you in his arms and offering you physical comfort. Stress that marriage is also a bargain. We are sure he expects you to 'scratch his back' in any one of a number of different ways – or does he do *all* his own washing, cooking, cleaning and shopping? And if he's so keen on masturbation, what's to stop him from tendering this simple service to you as a token of his esteem?

Q My lover has been unfaithful. When my husband did this to me in the past, I compensated by having an affair of my own – with my lover! Now I'm 60, retaliation doesn't seem feasible, but I'm so angry I don't know what to do.

A So you are saying that possibly for the first time in your life you must absorb the full shock and sadness of romantic rejection without recourse to revenge? If this really is a 'first', you can't possess many defences or resources against it. Learning is always painful, but you are going to have to do some. We don't know whether things can be patched up with your lover, or have been with your husband, but the little girl in you must now probe herself instead of bending the rest of the world to order. At its simplest, with whom are you going to share your melancholy fury? Whom will you tell?

Q **My husband had a heart attack last year. He has been told that regular sexual activity is actually good for him but he's terrified of giving it a go.**

A That's because there are so many poor jokes about older men dying in their lovers' arms. Show him this answer and do the following test. Get him to walk up at least twenty stairs at a moderate pace. So long as he isn't seriously out of breath at the top, assure him he is easily fit enough to make love to you. In fact, he has just undergone a *greater* physical exertion than the effort involved in performing sexual intercourse. It is also true that sex provides the most therapeutic exercise for the muscle tissue of the heart, and we don't imagine it will do you much harm either. By all means use woman-on-top positions if he would like to be extra cautious. One word of warning. Research does show that *extra-marital* sex carries an increased risk of cardiac arrest although most researchers attribute this to guilt, not exertion.

Q My wife has always been very independent
and our marriage has been punctuated by
separations during which few questions were
asked. But this year she became ill and
instead of looking 45 she's looking all her 59
years. She's become clingy, won't leave my
side and constantly wants sex.

A She is actually asking whether you are willing to
provide the emotional security she previously
obtained from youthful good looks and animal
energy. You don't need to become her sexual teddy
bear, in fact decline truly unwelcome sexual
advances, but just let her know whether you are
going to stand by her. She is having to cope
overnight with an ageing process most of us find
difficult to deal with in years. If you do offer this
reassurance, be prepared to repeat yourself
because, like a child, she may not 'hear' your
words at the outset.

Q **My wife has been told she ought to have a
mastectomy. I'm worried she'll be worried
about my reaction to this.**

A And maybe you are also plain worried – about the
operation itself, and about your own post-
operative responses? First, today's surgeons avoid
using this operation unless there is no alternative
so ensure you are both reconciled to its necessity.
Second, be careful to attend the pre-operation
conferences so you can give your wife all possible
support while adjusting yourself to the progress of
treatment. Third, you may find it helpful to see
your wife's scar for the first time in the presence
of the doctor. Fourth, women often feel despair at
undergoing such surgery as well as loss of
femininity so stroking, kissing and cuddling are
especially important during the first days of
convalescence. Last, when healing has occurred, it
would be symbolically reassuring if you could
deliberately include the area of the scar for
attention during lovemaking.

Q **My husband has to take several pills to counteract high blood pressure, but as a result of his illness he's become impotent. Would sex therapy help us?**

A Almost certainly it is the anti-hypertensive drugs your husband has been prescribed which have caused the change in his sexual response, so you really need to go back to the doctor to enquire about possible alternative medication. However, if given a choice between risking impotence or thrombosis, most men reluctantly select the former. Even so, don't give up sex just because sex has given up on erections. It may even be possible for your husband to ejaculate without erection (particularly if you massage his prostate) and all his penile sensations should remain a pleasure.

Q **My husband has always been a bit over-sexed. As a young man this was part of his charm – he was always trying it on. But now he's 71, it is causing problems. He's just like a dirty old man. The other day, he put his hand up the skirt of our 19-year-old cleaner and she promptly gave notice.**

A Unless he's suffering from Alzheimer's disease (where senility may result in uncontrolled sexual arousal) you can treat him like anyone else who refuses to abandon anti-social behaviour. Perhaps you might warn him that it remains open to your former cleaner to lay charges against him for indecent assault? Perhaps he gets to clean the living room himself? Certainly, he experiences the irritable edge of your tongue. Perhaps you both re-negotiate your sexual contract (also known as marriage) to include greater opportunities for sex?

Q A couple of years back, my husband began to have problems with sex. His erections became unreliable and his ejaculation lost its propulsive force. The doctor has diagnosed diabetes but the treatment hasn't solved the sex problem. In fact I can't get a straight answer out of my GP about our sexual prospects.

A He or she is 'waiting to see'. Unfortunately, diabetes comes in several forms with different consequences. In general, it impairs sexual function and is almost certainly responsible for your husband's present sexual difficulties. However, some patients regain full powers; some regain partial powers; some vary, and some continue to feel impotent. If your doctor falsely says 'this is what's going to happen for sure', then those very words will influence the outcome. (We presume you'd lose sexual confidence if told by an authority you could never have another orgasm?) On the other hand, the doctor cannot win since *not* giving you an answer also creates anxiety.

The best course is to start a conventional 'Masters and Johnson style' sex-therapy programme over several weeks in the privacy of your own home. You agree not to try intercourse. You both do massages and pleasuring treatments, first non-genitally, later graduating to include the genitals. You give feedback on how the strokes feel. You may eventually reach the point of wishing to 'stuff' his non-erect penis into your vagina, just to enjoy feeling sexually close, then lie back so that any of his psychological anxiety about 'penetration' can be allayed. At the same time, your husband should follow the paradoxical command 'Don't try to get an erection', to remove all pressure from the situation. If erection eventually returns, intercourse may be resumed with the woman on top or astride. If it doesn't,

continue with manual pleasuring. You may not
feel this is a complete substitute for intercourse
but it is a very delightful alternative.

Q I am a 65-year-old clergyman in an unhappy
marriage which I cannot leave. I'm desperate
for a relationship with an understanding
woman but I realize I'm no longer a great
catch. Sex with a prostitute is out of the
question. Why cannot women realize that
older men make the best lovers instead of
being so prejudiced against them?

A We've every sympathy with your dilemma but you
do seem to be suggesting that the rest of the
world should accommodate itself to your wishes.
In effect, you are faced with three tough choices –
Duty v Separation; Ethics v Adultery; Morality v
Paid Sex. Is there an option you think we've
missed?

Q **My husband has been told he must have a prostate operation. I have heard that this can result in loss of sexual ability. Is this true?**

A Most men find their prostate gland gets larger with age and some that the pressure on the urethral tube interferes with normal urination and ejaculation. In cases of gross enlargement, there are at least four ways for surgeons to tackle the necessary operation. The first three (transurethral, suprapubic and retropubic) should not interfere with physical sexual arousal at all. However, in these three cases, orgasm will appear to be 'dry' with any sperm or fluid being ejaculated 'backwards' into the bladder, rather than forwards out of the end of the penis. The least commonly performed (perineal) operation, on the other hand, invariably disturbs the nerve tissue leading to the penis rendering erection and ejaculation impossible.

Q **I am 66. My wife is 56. Her recent lack of desire for sex has distressed me, but I am far more bothered by the physical changes she's undergone – excess weight, hair falling out, always complaining about the cold, total lethargy and hours stuck in the loo. Are these normal signs of sudden ageing?**

A Not at 56, they're not. They are the classic symptoms of hypothyroidism and can be successfully treated with thyroxin.

Q My wife still turns me on every day despite 30 years of marriage but I am finding it more and more difficult to ejaculate.

A This is almost certainly an age-related development, the partial remedy for which is to increase the level of stimulation (both fantasy and friction) offered to you during lovemaking. The fantasies we'll leave to you (though legal erotica might well be worth contemplating). For increased friction, we suggest you try placing a pillow under your wife's buttocks in the missionary position so that downward pressure is exerted on your penis by your own body weight. Alternatively, ask your wife to clamp her legs together under your body during intercourse so that thigh pressure is added to maximum vaginal stimulation.

Q I never got much from sex with my first husband but now I'm going out with a man to whom I am very attached. Is it too late for a woman of 63 who has effectively been frigid for years?

A The New York sex therapist Betty Dodson used to describe her job satisfaction as 'being able to help a woman of 60 experience orgasm for the first time'. Sheila Kitzinger, the anthropologist, quotes the case of a woman who was anorgasmic through two marriages, began to have extra-marital relations at 72 and had her first orgasm at 74. There is also some physical evidence to support the folklore assumption that after spellbound years in a lonely bed, Sleeping Beauty could wake to perform wonderful sex with the Prince of her dreams 'just like that'. Women's bodies do seem able to 'come into flower' despite many years of winter.

Q Over the past few years my wife has become crippled by arthritis. She is embarrassed to ask the doctor about it, but her hips are a real problem during sex.

A And we're sure they are very painful too. Try to get her to talk to her doctor, perhaps by accompanying her to the surgery. Drugs can relieve much of the pain but also beneficial is a warm bath taken just prior to intercourse. Perhaps she'd like you to run this for her as well as bathe her? You should also find out which is her least painful time of day, because this can vary considerably. When hip-movement is too difficult, it might be better for you to switch to oral sex.

Q I live in a senior citizens' housing complex of a very sophisticated type. There are common rooms, communal social activities, even a swimming pool. I am 75 and realize that Molly, a 66-year-old widow, is falling for me. I'd love to remarry but know my sex life died years ago. Is it fair to expect her to marry me knowing we can't make love?

A Read the rest of this book. Then ask Molly.

Q **My husband has just returned from hospital after having an ileostomy operation. He now comes equipped with a little bag into which his waste continually drains. We've overcome most of the problems connected with this except when thinking about sex. If we make love, he's terrified it will smell – or that it will leak.**

A Well, let's be frank, these eventualities may occur so you need to be practically prepared. First, the doctor will give you a date for sexual resumption. Second, make sure the appliance is emptied prior to any sexual activity. Third, use sexual positions where pressure is diverted from the stoma site. Fourth, bolster your bodies with towels in case of accident. Fifth, be prepared to take far more of the sexual initiative than you may be used to, particularly in the early days, so that your husband can get accustomed to modifying his movements. Thousands of stoma operations are carried out each year and tens of thousands of couples continue with a happy sex life. Eventually, they stop thinking about the bag at all.

Q **My wife died a year ago and I mourn her a lot. She could never be replaced and I will never remarry. Lately, however, I've been experiencing some violently erotic dreams. Why?**

A Because although mourning needs to take place, sometimes for months and years, physical life goes on, including that to do with sexual desire. Moreover, the complexities of grief may cause you to feel anger that she has 'left' you as well as 'relief' that you are free. These could also feed into your fantasy dream life.

Q If a man wakens with an early morning erection does it mean he ought to be able to have intercourse? My 58-year-old husband had a minor stroke six months ago, manages these early morning stands but apparently cannot make love to me.

A It used to be believed that early morning erection was caused by a full bladder. Now we know that a full bladder and early morning erection are unrelated, except that the erection must subside before the urinary valve will open. What actually happens is that during the rapid eye movement phase of sleep, both men and women have their sexual systems automatically aroused. Both sexes, in fact, exhibit erections. If you waken while dreaming, you will probably notice this, although for reasons of size the man's condition will be more easily observed.

This physical response has diagnostic value for the sex therapist. The *absence* of early morning erection during dream sleep would tend to show that there are neurological or vascular debilities. The *partial absence* of erection might indicate blood leakage within the veinous system. And, as in your husband's case, despite his medical troubles, the *presence* of sustained early morning erection would tend to show that his physical equipment is fully functioning. Now this does not mean to say that he *wants* to have sex with this early morning hard-on. The sexual world is usually divided into larks and owls. But if he avoids intercourse at any time of day or night, it suggests he is either terrified of having a further stroke or he is simply avoiding sex with you. We think the former is more likely although your fears tend towards the latter. Now it's time to ask *him*.

Q I am a 42-year-old woman who has recently become engaged to a lovely 75-year-old man. Friends say I'm doomed to instant celibacy. I know his expectation of life is not enormous but what is the expectation of our sex life together?

A A 1926 bio-statistician, Raymond Pearl, found that four per cent of males aged 70-79 had intercourse every third day and another 9 per cent were having it weekly. In 1959, Dr A. L. Finkle and team questioned 101 men between the ages of 56 and 86 with no illness likely to reduce potency. He found that 65 per cent of the under-69s, and 34 per cent of the over 70s were still sexually active while almost half those aged 80 or over managed at least ten copulations per year. In the group which interests you, those aged over 70, the principal reason given for sexual inactivity was lack of desire (or partner), not incapacity. Of all the men aged over 65, only three said they could never have an erection. A third study by Newman and Nichols in 1960 questioned both sexes aged between 60 and 93. Of those aged between 75 and 90-plus, a quarter continued to have sexual relations. Again it was illness mainly accounting for the remainder's celibacy.

Q   My 62-year-old husband stopped having sex
with me after 35 years of happy marriage.
Now I've found what I suspect to be semen
stains on his underwear. Could he be having
an affair after all this time?

A   He does appear to have had a climax but we can't
tell under what circumtances. Your anxiety leads
you to suspect infidelity. Have you other evidence
for your suspicions? What's wrong with supposing
he's had some sort of wet dream or indulges in
private masturbation? Even so, perhaps you could
seize this opportunity to re-open the question of
your lapsed love-life? You do seem to let him take
all the decisions.

Q   I retired six months ago from a senior
executive position in industry. Since then my
sex life has gone to pot. I suppose I ought to
accept that there's a connection?

A   It could well be so, but it's sensible to get checked
for heart, circulation and nerve disorders first.
Ask your GP to run tests. Then if all the results
are negative, go on to consider whether retirement
might have produced a 'masked depression', the
most likely alternative explanation for what's
gone wrong.

Q I'm a married man of 64. My erections aren't all that powerful and I find on the whole I prefer to masturbate alone rather than attempt intercourse with my spouse.

A Well, we register your preference and would make no comment were you single. But you remind us of the story about the aristocrat and the butler – The Aristocrat: 'Jeeves, I've got another erection!' Butler: 'Shall I tell her ladyship, my lord?' The Aristocrat: 'No, Jeeves, I think we'll smuggle this one up to London.' Aren't you really withholding yourself from your partner, partly because of embarrassment, partly because of possible disaffection? So long as you are both happy, it doesn't matter. But *are* you?

Q I am an 87-year-old widower who masturbates every day. Will it do me any harm?

A On the contrary – despite what you must have been taught about 'going blind' and 'getting hairs on the palm of your hand' when you were growing up in the 1900s.

Q I'm a widow of 64 and keep reading of dire health consequences if I don't maintain a fulfilling sex life. My difficulty is that I don't have or want a sex life. Gardening gives me more pleasure.

A Then gardening it shall be. If there were truth in these rumours we should expect nunneries to be full of the halt, the lame, the sick and the prematurely deceased, would we not? What does damage health is a life of psychosexual frustration, a different dilemma altogether.

Index